Arguably Contentious

Arguably Contentious

Thoughts on a Divided World

M. HAMID ANSARI

RUPA

Published by
Rupa Publications India Pvt. Ltd 2026
7/16, Ansari Road, Daryaganj
New Delhi 110002

Sales centres:
Bengaluru Chennai Hyderabad
Jaipur Kathmandu Kolkata
Mumbai Prayagraj

P-ISBN: 978-93-5352-849-2
E-ISBN: 978-93-5352-385-5

First impression 2026

10 9 8 7 6 5 4 3 2 1

Printed in India

For
Salma,
Sulaiman, Nuriya, Osman

Hasti ke mat fareb men aa jaiyo 'asad'
Aalam tamaam halqa-e-dam-e-khyal hai

(O Asad: Do not be prey to the deceptions of existence
for the entire world is only a trap of illusions)

Contents

PART II
ZONES OF TURBULENCE

Preface

Aspe laghar miya ba-kar aayad
Roze maidan na gao parwari

(On the day of battle the slender steed is useful,
and not the fattened ox.[1])

Hence also the need to appreciate the wisdom of a latter-day publicist: 'Fear not those who argue but those who dodge.' These essays, written at different times in recent years, deal with a principal concern: the sociopolitical direction of our society. In addition, a second set of essays, without additional commentary, deal with some problems in the wider world that unavoidably influence our existence in the global community.

THE MEANING AND CONTOURS OF FRATERNITY IN OUR SOCIETY

At home, my principal concern is the sociopolitical direction of our society. The debate on it was evident in the Constituent Assembly and continues to this day. For domestic political reasons, it has acquired intensity.

Swaraj was the sacred and practical objective of the Freedom Movement. In 1924, Gandhi had written: 'By Swaraj I mean the government of India by the consent of the people as ascertained by the largest number of the adult population…real Swaraj will come not by the acquisition of authority by a few, but by the

---

[1]Gulistan of Shaikh Sa'di. Story 3. *The Manners of Kings.*

acquisition of the capacity by all to resist authority when it is abused.'[2]

On this basis and even before joining the Constituent Assembly, Dr Ambedkar was developing ideas of constitutional theory and democracy. In *Annihilation of Caste* (1936), he wrote, 'My ideal would be a society based on Liberty, Equality and Fraternity, which is only another name for democracy. Democracy is not merely a form of Government. It is primarily a mode of associated living, of conjoint communicated experience. It is essentially an attitude of respect and reverence towards fellowmen.'[3]

However, while prescribing a set of basic individual and group rights for the people of India, an essential ingredient relating to their relationship with each other in their daily lives was insufficiently considered. This was pointed out by the Chairman of the Drafting Committee Dr B.R. Ambedkar in its concluding session on 25 November 1949 when he drew attention to the principle of fraternity: What does fraternity mean? 'Fraternity means a sense of common brotherhood of all Indians—of all Indians being one people. It is the principle which gives unity and solidarity to social life. It is a difficult thing to achieve...'[4]

He added elsewhere that 'without fraternity, equality and liberty will be no deeper than coats of paint'[5]; that fraternity has been most forgotten in our Constitution and in our electoral process, that, in turn, is reproduced in our hearts and homes. The idea of fraternity is closely linked to that of social solidarity, which is impossible to accomplish without public empathy.

---

[2]Gandhi, M.K., 'What Swaraj Means to Me', *The Mind of Mahatma Gandhi*, R.K. Prabhu and Rao (eds.), Oxford University Press, London, 1946, pp. 317–322.

[3]Ambedkar, Dr Bhimrao, *Annihilation of Caste: The Annotated Critical Edition*, Navayana, New Delhi, 2015.

[4]'Constituent Assembly Debates, Vol. 11, 25 November 1949', *Constitution of India*, https://tinyurl.com/56jyfwu3. Accessed on 25 September 2025.

[5]Ibid.

Despite this, there was little discussion in the Assembly. Only Acharya Kripalani, on 17 October 1949, drew attention to its implications and pointed out that the principles of the Preamble were not only legal and political principles, but they also had a moral, spiritual and mystical content:

'If we want to use democracy as only a legal, constitutional and formal device, I submit, we shall fail [...] the whole country should understand the moral, the spiritual and the mystic implication of the word democracy [...] If we have not done that, we shall fail as they have failed in other countries. Democracy will be made into autocracy and it will be made into imperialism, and it will be made into fascism. But as a moral principle, it must be lived in life. If it is not lived in life, and the whole of it in all its departments, it becomes only a formal and a legal principle.'

The ambit of the principle notwithstanding, the only mention of the concept is in the Preamble where, along with Justice, Liberty and Equality, Fraternity 'assuring dignity of the individual and unity and integrity of the Nation' is mentioned.

An aspect of the concept also emerged in John Rawls's observation that 'justice is the first virtue of social institutions' and that 'rights secured by justice are not subject to political bargaining or to the calculus of social interests.' This, to him, provided an interpretation of the principle of fraternity 'even though it has a lesser place in democratic theory' and 'imposes a definite requirement on the basic structure of society.'

The idea of fraternity and brotherhood, but not the terms themselves, figures (after the 42nd Amendments) in Article 51A(e) of the Constitution where amongst the duties of citizens is mentioned the duty 'to promote harmony and the spirit of common brotherhood among all the people of India transcending religious, linguistic and regional or sectional diversities, to renounce practices derogatory to the dignity of women.' Despite this, the principle has been used infrequently in practice.

What duties then should emanate from it? The wording of 51A(e) does not go beyond what Sir Ernest Barker called an emotion or a sentiment. Fraternity, he wrote, 'is a dubious word which may be used to denote both emotion and principle but is perhaps generally used to denote emotion rather than principle [...] the emotion of loyalty to state and the emotion of loyalty to the state and the emotion of national society are, or should be,, controlled emotions.'[6]

For this reason, as Rajeev Bhargava has argued, there is 'a pressing need to excavate the moral values embedded in the Constitution, to bring out their connections, and to identify the coherent or not-so coherent worldviews contained within it.'[7]

The aspiration of the text of the Preamble of the Constitution thus emerges as (a) liberty and equality, (b) dignity and justice, and (c) fraternity, liberty and equality. Ambedkar referred to this trio as the foundations of an ideal society.

To what extent have we achieved them?

THE BASE OF ALL

Part IV of the Constitution highlights the dilemma of policymaking. The Directive Principles of State Policy and particularly Articles 37 and 38 state that they shall not be enforceable by any court but are nevertheless fundamental to the governance of the country and it shall be the duty of the State to apply them in making laws. Article 51A prescribes the Fundamental Duties, and part (e) of it prescribes the duty 'to promote harmony and the spirit of common brotherhood amongst all the people of India transcending religious, linguistic and

[6]Barker, Sir Ernest, *Principles of Social and Political Theory*, Oxford University Press, Oxford, 1952.

[7]'Govt of NCT of Delhi vs Union of India', *Supreme Court Observer*, p. 10, https://tinyurl.com/yc566xn6. Accessed on 25 September 2025.

regional or sectional diversities: to renounce practices derogatory to the dignity of women.'

None of these is prescriptive in a legal sense and their observance in governance would therefore depend on public sense of the day and their expression in electoral judgements in national or local elections.

And so, while several governments over the past seven and a half decades have dedicated themselves to the objective in varying measure, the result of their effort is to be sought in the score cards of the results in quantitative terms, as reflected in national and global elections and in informed studies where it is argued that 'while democratic mobilization has produced an intense struggle for power, it has not delivered millions of citizens from the abject dictates of poverty.'

Thus, the de jure 'WE, the People' in the first line of the Preamble is in reality a fragmented 'we', divided by yawning gaps that remain to be bridge, and show that 'unequal economic opportunities lead to unequal outcomes which in turn lead to unequal access to political power, and all these result in persistence of initial conditions.'[8]

Some years after the drafting of the text of the Constitution, Ambedkar spoke on the limitations of the exercise of democracy in a speech in the Constituent Assembly on 22 December 1952 where he dwelt on what he called 'Conditions Precedent for the Successful Working of Democracy'. He listed these as absence of glaring inequalities; presence of an opposition; quality of law and administration; observance of constitutional morality; avoidance of tyranny of majority over minority; a functioning of moral order in society; and public conscience[9].

[8]Ansari, Hamid, *Challenges to a Liberal Polity: Human Rights, Citizenship and Identity*, Penguin Viking, New Delhi, 2021, pp. xiii–xviii.

[9]Ambedkar, Dr Bhimrao, 'Conditions Precedent for the Successful Working of Democracy', *Writings and Speeches*, Vol.17, Part III, Ministry of Social Justice

Political democracy, he said, must transform into social democracy. 'These principles of liberty, equality and fraternity are not to be treated as separate items in a trinity. They form a union of trinity in the sense that to divorce one from the other is to defeat the very purpose of democracy. Liberty cannot be divorced from equality, equality, equality cannot be divorced from liberty. Nor can liberty and equality be divorced from fraternity. Without equality, liberty would produce the supremacy of the few over the many. Equality without liberty would kill individual initiative. Without fraternity, liberty and and equality could not become a natural course of things. It would require a constable to enforce them.'[10]

Where does this take fraternity? Article 51A(e) of the Constitution does not differentiate between citizens on any of the categories mentioned above and makes it an all-encompassing duty. Its ambit therefore is universal; its observance, by the same logic, has to begin at the base of the ladder of citizenship rather than the top, but does not spare the leadership from the obligation to promote and practise it.

JUDGING THE PRAXIS

Has this been done in practice?

Over time, uneven development has characterized the states of the Indian Union. Regional and linguistic diversity characterizes them; so does uneven economic development and progress, resulting in uneven levels of education, employment, social cohesion and contentment.[11]

---

and Empowerment, p. 510.

[10]Ibid.

[11]Ansari, Hamid, 'The Ambit of Fraternity and the Wages of Oblivion', *The Hindu*, 22 September 2022, https://tinyurl.com/yc7w3uwm. Accessed on 25 September 2025.

The record is depressing; hence the ease with which non-fraternal patterns of behaviour seem to emerge in our society's practice. How often have social and political leaders of opinion promoted fraternity, incidentally or specifically, locally, within the region or nationally?

Judicial practice in the Supreme Court has at times used the concept of fraternity. An academic analysis has opined that 'the Court has advocated the use of the Preamble only in those situations where the provisions of the Constitution under consideration are ambiguous, and the Preamble may be used to aid in the removal of such ambiguity. If, however, there is no uncertainty as to the meaning, purpose or scope of the provision the Preamble would have no role to play in the interpretation.'[12]

Seventy-five years on, a candid assessment of the state of the Republic makes us cogitate on evidence of regional diversity, assertion of linguistic identity, and emergence of diverging political orientations. While the first two are physical and social realities, the third is a product of thriving diversity. Each is real, each is also disconcerting from the viewpoint of federal governance hitherto practised, and each seeks accommodation in a divergent framework.

In a comprehensive analysis, Aakar Patel has examined the coverage of India in 16 global assessment agencies and, for added effect, reproduced the results graphically on front and rear covers.[13] These depict India as a 'flawed democracy', as 'partly free', and in HDI indicators.

Does this promote national integration, rhetoric apart? The dominant political imagery of the freedom movement was

---

[12]Shetty, Smaran, and Tanaya Sanyal, 'Fraternity and the Constitution: A Promising Beginning in Nandini Sundar V. State of Chattisgarh', *NUJS Law Review*, Vol. 439, 2011, pp. 439–462, https://tinyurl.com/5y9dcdha. Accessed on 25 September 2025.

[13]Patel, Aakar, *Price of the Modi Years*, Penguin Vintage Books, 2021, pp. 11–48.

civic-national in form. This in recent years, in the words of Professor Niraja Jayal, has been replaced in form by a new 'political imagery of ethno-religious majoritarianism', one having a distinctive new form of citizenship that signals 'a possibly irreversible damage to India's organically consensual social fabric.'[14]

Ambedkar had rightly anticipated 'a life of contradictions' for our times and the past seven decades have shed much light on the veracity of his prediction.

GLASS HALF FULL

Today we have to concede that the glass of democracy remains half full. We have practised electoral democracy mechanically without making it fully representative. Our electoral procedures and practices have accentuated rather than diminished these deviations.

We have yet to succeed in eradicating electoral malpractices. We have allowed money power in all its manifestations to distort electoral outcomes and failed to make them free and fair. Our political process depicts ideological decadence and a declining observance of constitutional morality. Our society exhibits a declining disregard for moral order and public conscience.

Similarly, developing tendencies of majoritarianism and weaponization of history to target specific segments of the citizen body have aggravated social cleavages.

Two questions that loom large on the political horizons relate to (a) language and (b) delimitation.

The argument about *rajbhasha* and the adverse reaction to it in some of the states is on the grounds that it is official, *not* national, and that all the 22 languages in the Eighth Schedule have

---

[14]Jayal, Niraja Gopal, *Re-forming India: The Nation Today*, Penguin Viking, Gurgaon, 2019.

an official status. It is also felt that Article 351 by its wording is of a general recommendatory nature, more so because Hindustani is neither included in the Schedule nor is its role defined.

Similarly, the argument about delimitation on the basis of Article 82 overlooks the fact that barring the general election of 1971, others have not followed the census rule. It has been argued, and justifiably so, that the bonds of national unity would be strengthened if there is a permanent freeze on the reallocation of parliamentary seats since it would help secure the Indian Union against challenges to the bonds of national unity emanating from cultural, economic and cultural fault lines and possible political hegemony.

An aggravating factor is the shape that inequality takes in different segments of our society. It is economic on one plane; on others it is regional, casteist and religious. Some are spelt out, others understated, still others assumed. Sociologists have identified nine categories of people who are determined to be socially and/or politically and/or economically excluded. These particularly include Dalits, Adivasis, women and religious minorities.

Recent studies on religious minorities who constitute approximately 20 per cent of India's population have traced discrimination relating to them to perceptions that relate to the very origins of thinking that brought about the Partition of August 1947. They argue that violence was not merely accidental but integral to the foundation of the nation and that the need for fraternity coexisted with the imperative need for restoring order. This has been written about on the basis of the documentation made available subsequently and, at this distance of time, its validity cannot be dismissed altogether for social cohesion in segments of society.

ENHANCE AND EXPAND

A concomitant of fraternity is secularism. One of the matters in the societal domain that figures prominently in public discourse relates to the constitutional ideal of India being a 'secular' republic having a 'composite culture'. The former expression is in the Preamble and the latter in Article 51A(f).

Any discussion of these constitutional values has to be premised on the existential reality of our society. It is characterized by heterogeneity; a population of 1.3 billion comprising over 4,635 communities, 78 per cent of whom are not only linguistic and cultural but social categories. Religious minorities constitute 19.4 per cent of the total.[15] A poet expressed it finely in a couplet:

Ilahi lutf kya aata jo sub mai-khwar hi hote
Teri dunya ki raonaq barh gai sheikh o barahman se

Our democratic polity and its secular state structure were put in place in full awareness of this plurality. There was no suggestion to erase identities and homogenize them.

Political scientists and sociologists have written a good deal on the Indian perception of secularism. The three generally accepted characteristics of a secular state, namely liberty to practise religion, equality between religions as far as state practice is concerned, and neutrality or a fence of separation between the state and religion, have been invoked but 'their application has been contradictory and has led to major anomalies.' Commenting on the debate on secularism, Amartya Sen has observed that 'secularism is basically a demand for symmetric political treatment of different religious communities' but that leaves open 'the choice between the forms that symmetry can legitimately take'. He added that 'there is a real difference between achieving symmetry through the sum-total of

[15]'Religious Minorities in India Report', Council on Minority Rights in India, November 2022, https://tinyurl.com/c4da8xnj. Accessed on 24 September 2025.

the collective intolerances of the different communities rather than through the union of their respective tolerances.' Very recently, Soli Sorabjee has reminded us of Emmanuel v. State of Kerala and of Justice Chinappa Reddy's remarks on the subject of tolerance.

The challenge, then, is to reduce if not eliminate these anomalies.

This leads us to the question: how has the Indian state, in principle and practice, given shape to the essential ingredients of the secular principle and composite culture?

Apart from the principles enshrined in the constitutional text and policy pronouncements of public figures, often nuanced to suit the occasion, judicial pronouncements shed useful light on the matter.

The Basic Structure doctrine relating to our Constitution is now settled law. One of its ingredients is secularism. This is accepted in principle by most segments of opinion (barring advocates of some version of theocracy). It is more than a passive attitude of religious tolerance; it is a positive concept of equal treatment. Its most emphatic assertion in a pronouncement came in the set of judgements in the Bommai case:

> Secularism has both positive and negative contents. The Constitution struck a balance between temporal parts confining it to the person professing a particular religious faith or belief, and allows him to practice, profess and propagate his religion, subject to public order, morality and health. The positive part of secularism has been entrusted to the State to regulate by law or by an executive order. The State is prohibited to patronize any particular religion as State religion and is enjoined to observe neutrality. The State strikes a balance to ensure an atmosphere of full faith and confidence among its people to realize full growth of personality and to make him a rational being on secular lines,

> to improve individual excellence, regional growth, progress and national integrity... Religious tolerance and fraternity are basic features and postulates of the Constitution as a scheme for national integration and sectional or religious unity. Programmes or principles evolved by political parties based on religion amount to recognizing religion as a part of the political governance which the Constitution expressly prohibits. It violates the basic features of the Constitution. Positive secularism negates such a policy and any action in furtherance thereof would be violative of the basic features of the Constitution.[16]

The principle so laid down is emphatic. Despite its clarity, however, different interpretations were placed on it and 'there is no real consensus within the Court on what secularism entails.' It has been opined that what the Court said is different from what it did. Observers have noted that subsequent pronouncements of the Supreme Court have 'effectively vindicated the profoundly anti-secular vision of secularism' in some quarters. For this reason, it has been argued 'whether a more complete separation of religion and politics might not better serve Indian democracy.'[17]

The difficulty lies in delineating, for purposes of public policy and practice, the line that separates them from religion. For religion per se, and each individual religion figuring in the discourse, has to be defined in terms of its stated tenets. The 'way of life' argument, used in philosophical texts and some judicial pronouncements, does not help the process of identifying common principles of equity in a multi-religious society. Since a wall of separation is not possible under Indian

---

[16]S.R. Bommai vs Union of India, (1994) 3 SCC (Jour) 1, 11 March 1994, para 252. Also, paras 153(viii), 176, 177, 304, 434(10).

[17]Sen, Ronojoy, *Articles of Faith: Religion, Secularism and the Indian Supreme Court (Law in India)*, Oxford University Press, New Delhi, 2010, p. xxix.

conditions, the challenge is to develop a formula for equidistance and minimum involvement. For this purpose, principles of faith need to be segregated from contours of culture since a conflation of the two obfuscates the boundaries of both and creates space to equivocation. Furthermore, such an argument could be availed of by other faiths in the land since all claim a cultural sphere and a historical justification for it.

Within the same ambit, but distinct from it, is the constitutional principle of equality of status and opportunity, amplified through Articles 14, 15 and 16. This equality has to be substantive rather than merely formal and has to be given shape through requisite measures of affirmative action needed in each case so that the journey on the path to development has a common starting point. The Kundu Report on Diversity Index in 2008 had drawn attention to the 'Inequality Traps' that keep the marginalized excluded and work in favour of the dominant groups in a society, and had concluded that 'unequal economic opportunities lead to unequal outcomes which in turn lead to unequal access to political power. This creates a vicious circle since unequal power structure determines the nature and functioning of the institutions and their policies. All these result in persistence of initial conditions.'[18]

DEFINING OUR CULTURE

The same absence of homogeneity holds good for 'composite culture'. The freedom movement recognized this existential reality of immense diversity on the ground. The Bommai judgement said that 'this cultural heritage in India shaped that people of all religious faiths, living in different parts of the country, are to

---

[18]Cossman, Brenda, and Ratna Kapur, 'Secularism: Bench-Marked by Hindu Right', *Economic and Political Weekly*, Vol. 31, No. 38, 1996, pp. 2613–30, https://tinyurl.com/awy9atn6. Accessed on 24 September 2025.

tolerate each other's religious faiths or beliefs and each religion made its contribution to enrich the composite Indian culture as a happy blend or synthesis.' Thus, secularism and composite culture are two sides of the same coin. A historian has analysed it in some detail:

> Social and cultural life in India incorporated within it a multi-regional and multi-religious form and content. This interpretation of cultural influences was neither uniform nor equally intense in all regions. Yet their presence is marked all over. As a result, although historically cultural transactions and social negotiations embraced the entire subcontinent, they led to variety and plurality rather than to homogeneity. In almost all realms of cultural production—music, drama, painting, architecture, and so on—as well as religion, different influences made their mark, imparting to them a composite character. As a result, historically, India developed as a colourful cultural mosaic and not as the manifestation of cultural practices inspired by a single source. The dynamism of Indian culture is derived from this diversity, which moulded the cultural practices of the people. It is in this sense that culture was embedded in national identity.
>
> The cultural implication of this historical process is not limited to diversity and plurality at the national level, but within each region itself as well […] The coming together of people of diverse cultural moorings and traditions had several cultural consequences. These have been variously conceived as synthesis, assimilation, acculturation, and eclecticism […] Whether India developed as a melting pot of cultures, or only remained a salad bowl is no more the issue. The crucial question is whether Indian culture is conceived as a static phenomenon, tracing its identity to

> a single unchanging source, or a dynamic phenomenon, critically and creatively interrogating all that is new.[19]

A primary concern of the makers of the Constitution was the cohesion and integration of the units of the new Republic formally described as 'a Union of States'. In the words of Sardar Vallabhbhai Patel, 'the inspiration and the stimulus came from above rather than from below and unless the transplanted growth takes a healthy root in the soil, there will be a danger of collapse and chaos.' This was amplified by V.P. Menon as the integration 'of the minds of the people'.

The challenge today is to invest our democracy with a moral content at the individual and societal level. It has to take the shape of an imperative; a failure to do so would expose us to the threat of fragmentation. It was rightly said many years ago: 'Fear not those who argue but those who dodge.'

Its consequences should not be guessed.

[19]Panikkar, K.N., *Colonialism, Culture, and Resistance*, Oxford University Press, New Delhi, 2007, p. 95.

PART I

POLITY

Chapter 1

A Democratic Diagnosis: Comatose or Torpid

An op-ed by CPM's Brinda Karat two days before the inauguration of the new Indian parliament summed up the emerging prospects succinctly: 'A parliamentary majority is being used as a bulldozer to fashion an autocracy, the new India version of a presidential form of governance [...] The replacement, at the forthcoming inaugural, of the real president of the Indian republic by the prime minister may symbolize more than the ego of an individual.'[1]

I had, some years back, read and put away Levitsky & Ziblatt's *How Democracies Die* that discusses the fate of democracies, happy in the thought that India did not find a mention in it. Little had I visualized a time when dexterous devices would be used in quest of the desired objective.

Our parliamentary system, crafted with some care, was sought to achieve (i) law-making, (ii) accountability of the executive, (iii) approval of taxation proposals and control of national finances, and (iv) discussion of matters of public interest and concern. India, it said, 'shall be a Union of States' and the provisions of Part XI of the Constitution would govern the relations between the Union and the states.

---

[1]Karat, Brinda, 'Opposition's boycott of inauguration of new Parliament is a form of democratic protest', *The Indian Express*, 26 May 2023, https://tinyurl.com/4ctn5mat. Accessed on 27 August 2025.

Ambedkar had emphasized that the eventual objective of social democracy was a trinity of liberty, equality and fraternity best achieved through the effective functioning of the Legislature, the Executive and the Judiciary. These foundational principles were spelt out in the Preamble of the Constitution and were reinforced by the Supreme Court in the Basic Structure doctrine.

CHANGING ORDERS

The challenge was in effective functioning of the principal ingredients, beginning with the first. Available data makes evident a progressive decline in its functioning year-wise, session-wise and decade-wise. It is clear that the parliament has lost its effectiveness as an instrument of scrutiny, accountability and oversight. Instead, devices of disruption crafted in Opposition and innocently disowned in government are sought to be legitimized. Above all, the leadership of the day endorses it by studied silence or lack of attendance or both, and with a noticeable tardiness towards the functioning of the Standing Committees. The end result is a declining process of scrutiny, debate and dissent. Periodic elections apart, informed opinion is concerned about its derailment and the resultant consequences. The emergence of social media, a rival claimant to representation in civil society, has emerged as both complementary and antithetical to question or supplement the representativeness of parliament. It has manifested itself in both forms in our polity. So, as a political scientist put it, 'while Parliament has become increasingly representative in descriptive terms, it also simultaneously becomes unresponsive in terms of legislation and governance and has tended to avoid accountability by closing ranks.'[2] An element of ideological orientation in the

[2]Sappal, Gurdeep Singh, and Pushparaj Deshpande (eds.), *The Great Indian Manthan: State, Statecraft and the Republic (Rethinking India Series Vol. 10)*, Penguin Random House India Private Limited, 2023.

shape of dharmic sanctification, as in the parliament ceremony, was used to reinforce it.

These moves suggest a design for centralization and personalization, and the creation of a 'Fuhrer or Zaeem-like' image not unknown in recent Indian history. Alongside, administrative devices have been sought to be used to bring in line state institutions having an impact on the electoral process. Both contributed to the achievement of transition from populism to electoral authoritarianism; both are violative of the spirit of the constitutional text.

One consequence of this trend, reflective of the unease generated by it, is a statement in the shape of a letter written to the President by a group of former civil servants expressing concern over attempts by the government to change the character of the civil service and its functioning, leading to the civil servants being 'torn between conflicting loyalties, thereby weakening their ability to be impartial'[3].

These trends in the changing character of the Indian polity have caused public concern and have not gone unnoticed by observers abroad. One editorial comment opined that 'Hindu nationalism in India is writing an epitaph for the country's experiment with multi-ethnic secular democracy.'[4] In his tome published last year, Christophe Jaffrelot has analysed the Hindutva ideology (laced with populism) based on Israeli scholar Sammy Smooha's theory of ethnic democracy which is defined as 'the ideology of a group that considers itself bound by racial, linguistic, religious or other cultural characteristics with a sense of superiority and rejection

[3]The Wire Staff, 'BJP Govt Making Systematic Effort to Change Character of Civil Services, Says Former Officers', *The Wire*, 25 May 2023, https://tinyurl.com/4snhhee7. Accessed on 27 August 2025.

[4]Editorial, 'The Guardian View on India at a Crossroads: Development, not Dictatorship', *The Guardian*, 24 April 2023, https://tinyurl.com/5cywe84r. Accessed on 27 August 2025.

of the "Other" generally perceived as a threat to the survival and integrity of the ethnic nation.'[5]

A NEW HEGEMONY

The conflation between nationalism and Hindutva has been the backbone of the new hegemony that has been of immense help to the BJP in projecting a potent conjoint image of Hindutva and development. That, as Suhas Palshikar has pointed out, 'is why the Bharatiya Janata Party has been so happy with intellectuals trying to problematize the nation. That particular intellectual initiative simultaneously places the BJP in a position of immense advantage and ensures that "anti-BJP" would necessarily be equated with the anti-national! Independently, both ideas—Hindutva and development—are potent political discourses. By weaving them together with nationalism, Narendra Modi has bound them into an arsenal of his political offensive.'[6]

This carefully calibrated personality cult with an image of infallibility has been reinforced by the publicity associated with India's presidency of G-20. The entire effort was to mesmerize the public, particularly the middle class, with the delusion of an image of India being the Vishwaguru at a time when the contrary is observed in the falling standards in educational institutions, in rising unemployment and its impact on public welfare.

The inauguration of the new building of parliament was noticeably devoid of any suggestions to make its functioning more meaningful. The formal equality of the two Houses seems to have been done away with and the Leader of the Lok Sabha

---

[5]Jaffrelot, Christophe, *Modi's India: Hindu Nationalism and The Rise of Ethnic Democracy*, Princeton University Press, 2021, p. 155.

[6]Palshikar, Suhas, 'India's Second Dominant Party System', *Economic and Political Weekly*, Vol. 52, No. 12, 2017, https://tinyurl.com/2z5rstm8. Accessed on 27 August 2025.

in his oration could have suggested, but did not, measures to increase the working days to 90–100 as in the past, initiate the practice of having a Prime Minister's Question Hour each week in both Houses, and proposed more effective measuring for the functioning of the Committee system to enhance its effectiveness and public confidence. More working space for the MPs could thus be justified in practice. No such suggestions however were forthcoming. So, will the new building contribute to a more functional and productive parliament? Will it enhance the democratic process in the polity? Will it, as the Prime Minister said in his inaugural speech, 'awaken the sense of duty in every Indian'[7] and include in it those who sit and work in the new structure and those who lead it in its primary duty? Would he recall to himself and his colleagues Ambedkar's December 1952 lecture on 'Conditions Precedent for the Successful Working of Democracy'[8]?

This article was originally published in The Hindu *on 7 June 2023, under the headline 'The Indian polity, a democratic diagnosis'.*

[7]Ministry of Culture, 'Union Home Minister and Minister of Cooperation, Shri Amit Shah, launched the Amrit Kalash Yatra under the 'Meri Maati-Mera Desh' campaign in New Delhi, today', *PIB Delhi*, 1 September 2023, https://tinyurl.com/5cvr7t62. Accessed on 27 August 2025.

[8]Ambedkar, Dr Bhimrao, 'Conditions Precedent for the Successful Working of Democracy', *Writings and Speeches Vol. 17, Part III—Dr Bhimrao Ambedkar and his Egalitarian Revolution-Speeches,* Dr Ambedkar Foundation, Ministry of Social Justice and Empowerment, https://tinyurl.com/5272x8ak. Accessed on 8 September 2025.

Chapter 2

Settling the Language for Cooperative Federalism

Cooperative federalism and 'cultural chauvinism'. The latter expression found mention in an editorial comment and bears repetition: 'This latest effort to impose Hindi raises once again and quite retrogressively the issue of cultural nationalism at a time when it is least required. India has remained uniquely unified despite the infinite multiplicities of its cultures…'

Language is an essential ingredient of identity. The question of expressing national identity in a linguistically diverse society anxious to jettison or reduce the use of English as the language of the colonial power was passionately debated by the makers of the Constitution and even linked to 'national prestige'. It was an uneasy compromise reflected in the wording of Part XVII (Articles 343–351).

SPELLING IT OUT

Article 345 leaves it to the state to choose its language for official purposes. In actual practice, several states and union territories continue to use English. Article 348 stipulates that all proceedings of the Supreme Court and 'of every High Court' and of Bills, etc., in parliament shall be in the English language.

The Eighth Schedule and the periodic additions to it (now numbering 22) spell out the diversity and complexity of the language landscape as do the Official Languages Act of 1963 and its Rules made in 1976 and amended in 1987, 2007 and 2011.

The question of official language brought forth 'passionate dissents' in the Constituent Assembly and the drafting of the Constitution. It covered language of legislatures, language of the courts and the judiciary, and language of the official work of the Union. Educational institutions of 'national importance' and those of 'scientific and technical education financed by Government of India' were in the Union List, and education 'including technical, medical and universities' were in the Concurrent List.

Some ambiguity inevitably crept into it. Thus Article 351 directs the state, in the development of Hindi, to draw upon other languages in the composite culture of India. These include Hindustani that does not find a mention in the Eighth Schedule.

A DISSENT THAT SURFACES FROM TIME TO TIME

This passionate dissent—beginning with the B.G. Kher Commission—continues to this day and surfaces from time to time. It assumed a violent form in 1965 in Tamil Nadu, where violent disturbances led to more than 50 deaths. In recent years, the reactions from the southern states, especially Tamil Nadu and Kerala, have been sharp and unambiguous. *The Hindu* reported on 27 November 2022 that 'an 85-year-old DMK functionary ended his life in Salem on Saturday' purportedly over the Central government's imposition of Hindi in Tamil Nadu.[9]

Unlike other parliamentary committees, the committee on official language, though consisting of 30 members of parliament, is headed by the Home Minister. Its mandate is to review the progress made in the use of Hindi for official purposes, and to make recommendations to increase the use of Hindi in

---

[9] *The Hindu* Bureau, '85-year-old DMK functionary in Salem Ends Life Alleging Hindi Imposition, *The Hindu*, 27 November 2022. https://tinyurl.com/2vksx7ma. Accessed on 27 August 2025.

official communications. It submits its report to the President of India, who forwards its recommendations to the two Houses.

It is understood that so far only the recommendations of the reports up to the ninth in the year 2010 have been forwarded to the Houses of Parliament. The 10th and 11th reports have been submitted to the President and are not in the public domain.

The Home Minister's press conference in October that announced the completion of the 11th Report highlighted some of its recommendations on language of instruction and examinations in technical courses. This touched off an animated debate on its resulting implications and its practicality in terms of the availability of standard books and course material, and of teachers qualified to communicate it adequately. A related matter is the competence in Hindi language of candidates undertaking examinations in it and competing in equal measure with those whose mother tongue it is.

At the root of the debate is the bigger question of identity in a diverse society. Nowhere is it suggested that diversity, including linguistic diversity, is to be subsumed within linguistic uniformity.

THE 'NATIONAL LANGUAGE' ISSUE

The allegation of 'cultural chauvinism' emanates from the apprehension that the transition of English and Hindi from being the official languages of the Union to Hindi becoming the national language and bringing this about through such procedural devices as the language of instruction and examination and of textbooks is detrimental to students whose mother tongue is not Hindi. Its implications for competitiveness in the job market are evident.

It is to be recalled that the language of the chapter on Official Language is definitive and limits itself to the language of the Union. It does not mention a national language. There is no mention of it in the section on Directive Principles of State Policy or of Fundamental Duties. In fact, Article 344(3) stipulates that 'the just claims and interests of persons belonging to the non-Hindi speaking areas in regard to the public services' shall be considered by the President.

In this context, what are the courses open to the federal government in the context of the zeal reflected in the Home Minister's remarks? The constitutional course would be to opt for the language of Article 345 that allows each Legislature the use of Hindi for all official purposes. This would hinge on electoral success in terms of the official programme of the party in power. Its absence, by the same token, would make the matter politically contentious, even acrimonious.

Would not such a course, if adopted, be prudent for political harmony implied in cooperative federalism in the long run, more so because English is now accepted as the language of discourse across continents, and its colonial past is a matter of distant history?

This article was originally published in The Hindu *on 30 November 2022, under the headline 'Settling the language for cooperative federalism'.*

Chapter 3

The Choice Is Narrowing the Circle or Widening It

An editorial comment recently opined 'India is witnessing the progressive normalization of minority baiting.' Some developments in a related context lend credence to it. Recent happenings within the country and their reactions in lands far and near tend to pose the problem. The sequencing is relevant and must not be interchanged. The reactions beyond our shores were not autonomous and were induced by what was said to audiences at home, by whom it was said, and why it became critical and induced reactions, immediate and over a passage of time.

One aspect of the matter, understandably played up in the domestic media, is the reaction in the Gulf Cooperation Council and Persian Gulf countries with whom India has extensive and diverse political and commercial relations. These also provide gainful employment to many million Indian nationals whose remittances are an important source of foreign exchange, in turn sustaining millions of households. Each of these has been quantified. In strategic terms, the region is India's extended neighbourhood; so is the case with Malaysia and Indonesia and Brunei in Southeast Asia.

It is evident that the malaise (while being domestic in its origin) has global dimensions. Its external manifestations are aggravated by modern means of communication. By the same logic, the correctives have to emanate in the context of domestic perceptions and practices.

AN EMERGING DISQUIET

Muslims are our largest religious minority, constituting 15.2 per cent of the total population and numbering over 200 million.[10] After Indonesia, Pakistan and Bangladesh, they constitute the largest Muslim group anywhere in the world. They are spread all over the country and are well integrated, but of late, signs of evident disquiet have been evident in all segments of the community.

The reason for this are the remarks uttered in media debates by two spokespersons of the ruling party reflecting on the personality of the Prophet. After a lapse of over a week of deafening silence, one of these persons was suspended and the membership of the second dispensed with. Both actions are viewed as inadequate by the community. No reaction has emanated from senior levels of government. The silence of institutional bodies such as the National Human Rights Commission of India and of the National Commission for Minorities is intriguing; so is the apparent reticence of the judiciary.

On the contrary, the use of strong-arm tactics and bulldozers to counter public demonstrations seeking firmer action against alleged culprits is suggestive of bias and has been aptly summed up in a candid editorial comment: '[...] there is little doubt that the demolitions amount to an abuse of power, a challenge to the rule of law and are inherently illegal due to the absence of due process or proportionality.'[11] Some observers have even opined that the bulldozer is an instrument to silence the minorities since

[10]TNN, 'Muslims are World's Fastest Growing Religious Group: Pew', *The Times of India*, 12 July 2025, https://tinyurl.com/2ffa3bc9. Accessed on 18 September 2025.

[11]'Bulldozer on the Loose: On Demolition of Property of Muslim activists', *The Hindu*, 16 June 2022, https://tinyurl.com/mvavmem2. Accessed n 02 September 2025.

its use in similar cases involving non-minority public is wanting.

What then could be the intent? Would it be to discipline, and thereby give rise to a feeling of denial with all its consequences?

The operative constitutional principle in social behaviour should be the promotion of equality and fraternity. In actual practice it is the contrary; this results in furtherance of hate by denigration. In an earlier period, this used to focus principally on regional types and linguistic expressions. This was found to be troublesome since retaliation in kind was often quick and in equal measure. The alternative was to denigrate faiths or socioreligious practices in competitive one-upmanship. An easy target in this was the numerous but socially and economically weaker segments that could even be mocked in terms of assumed backwardness. And, since most of our fellow citizens have reverence for traditional belief, 'experts' were soon discovered for these target areas. The public's addiction to popular television and its concocted levels of debate (premised on a preference for the brash and the articulate) invariably produces the desired results sought after in some sections.

INDIC VERSUS NON-INDIC

A categorizing segment of recent origin is the differentiation between Indic and non-Indic. This, put together with the existential diversity of faiths, seeks to divide fellow citizens between those who pursue Indic faiths, assumed to be of Indian origin, and those who subscribe to Christianity and Islam, allegedly of external import. The argument is premised on a certain reading of Indian history and the sociological issue is sought to be premised on what constitutes *Indianness*, ignoring that our society is 'a mosaic in which primordial cleavages both intersect and intermix with contemporary socioeconomic segments.'

This ideological effort, in a quest of 'purifying exclusiveness', is premised on our reading of history. A relevant question is whose history: of India defined in the period of British rule, or of India traditionally defined as Bharat? The latter would include many segments of southern Asia covered today by the South Asian Association for Regional Cooperation (SAARC) countries. Furthermore, in terms of what is sought to be presented as our history would also include parts of Afghanistan and even of Iran since the latter was depicted by M.S. Golwalkar as 'nothing but the base of Aryabhumi'. One consequence of this would be to categorize Ghazni, Khilji, Lodi, etc., not as foreign invaders but as domestic brigands who committed acts of loot and plunder and even succeeded in establishing kingdoms. Nor can the landmass of Bharat be described in terms of faith alone since there was a period of several centuries when Buddhism was the dominant religion. Furthermore, in the centuries when the rulers were Muslims, no effort seems to have been made to carry out mass conversions; on the contrary, the influence of Sufi saints was more pervasive.

The Indian reality of migrating groups seeking greener pastures since times immemorial qualifies our nomenclature of a 'civilizational state' and is better depicted in Raghupati Rai Firaq's couplet:

Sar zamin-e-hind par aqwam-e-alam ke Firaq
Qafile baste gae hindostan banta gaya[12]

(Caravans from nations of the world kept coming and contributed to the formation of Hindostan)

Linguistically, India has also been called 'a land of linguistic minorities'[13]. The Linguistic Survey of India and the research of Ganesh N. Devy bring forth the regional diversity of

[12]Firaq Gorakhpuri.

[13]Devy, Ganesh N., writings in *People's Linguistic Survey of India*, Orient Blackswan, 2014, New Delhi.

living languages. This lends credence to outbursts against linguistic homogeneity that is attempted periodically in the guise of national unity.

In multiple senses, our national choice thus lies in an ever-widening circle and in resisting all attempts, however well meaning, in abridging it. India is and must remain diverse and inclusive, and continue to build itself on the principles inscribed in the Preamble.

This article was originally published in The Hindu *on 21 June 2022, under the headline 'Narrowing the circle or widening it — choices for the polity'.*

Chapter 4

Bharat to India

'From Bharat to India' is an eye-catching title, obverse as it is to prevalent terminology. The author, a sociologist of eminence and a former president of International Association of Sociologists, Prof. T.K. Oommen, has described it as part two of his autobiographical essay the first section of which, 'Workography', was published some years back. This neat, albeit unusual, bifurcation of life over a lifetime sheds light on his thought process.

Over the years, Oommen has written extensively on the concept of social security and opined that the principal challenges to the evolution of a nation lie in minimizing disparity, eradication of discrimination and avoiding alienation. He has listed nine categories of socially and/or politically and/or excluded groups in our society: 'Dalits, Adivasis, OBCs, cultural minorities–both religious and linguistic, women, refugees-foreigners-outsiders, people of North-East India, the poor and the disabled,' and suggested that 'the three sources of exclusion in India—stratification, heterogeneity and hierarchy—operate conjointly and create intersectionality.'[14] This insecurity manifests itself in genocide, culturocide and ecocide, and in its absence a society may be conceptualized as secure.

---

[14]Oommen, T.K, 'Towards Building Inclusive Societies: Some Conceptual Clarificataions and Practical Suggestions with Special Reference to India', *Towards Inclusive Societies: Psychological and Sociological Perspectives*, Dharmendra Nath Tiwari (ed.), Routledge India.

The concluding sections of the present monograph are on the idea of India, and on 'the dichotomy of going beyond Bharat and India,' and on social formation and the moulding of individual identities. He dwells on the diversity of our social makeup and makes the telling point that while he could claim to be a Dravidian for 5,000 years, his identity as a Syrian Christian is traceable for two millennia and for six centuries as a Malayalam speaker. Each of this, he adds, coexists with his being an Indian for seven decades and, by the same token, qualifies the latter.

The absolutes are missing in this formulation. It accommodates complexity and sums it up succinctly. The Indian polity 'has the most elaborate set of identities based on class, religion, gender, caste, region, language and their intersectionalities as well as consequent permutations and combinations. To ignore this complex social set-up and speak in terms of "multiple identities" is not only simplistic but also misleading. And, given the long history of India and its shifting frontiers, it is not easy even to identify the identity markers of Indian citizens and demarcate the numerous identity groups in India.'[15]

A fruitful route forward, he suggests, would be to look at 'the major steps in the social formation of India.' Today this civilizational entity has several sovereign states within it and is geographically ambiguous. Within India the 'linguistic re-organization of States in the mid-1950s reinforced the idea of the Indian polity as a cultural coalition.'

These remarks suggest a relook at the contours of the current politically fashionable debate about unity in diversity and about social inclusion and exclusion. This does not seem to be happening; instead, as a reputable journal has put it this week, 'bulldozing the idea of India'[16] seems to have become the

[15]Ibid.

[16]Ramakrishnan, Venkitesh, 'Bulldozing the Idea of India,' *Frontline Magazine*, 1 May 2022, https://tinyurl.com/36kpdsyu. Accessed on 02 September 2025.

preferred option of those associated with the ruling circle.

This is neither desirable nor healthy for the polity and while there is endless talk of the Constitution and its edicts, the principles of liberty, justice, equality and fraternity that are intended to give unity and integrity to the nation are being sidestepped.

Recalling these principles compels us to revert to Ambedkar's last speech in the Constituent Assembly on 25 November 1949 and to his three warnings to ensure continuance of democracy 'not merely in form but also in fact.'[17] These were constitutional procedures, avoidance of hero worship, and social democracy instead of mere political democracy. The latter, Ambedkar emphasized, necessitates equality and fraternity.

Why then is the principle of fraternity absent from the pronouncements of leaders of opinion and those who set its direction and pace? What prevents them from emphasizing its centrality as visualized by Ambedkar? Its absence from writings and speeches, and from social media exchanges, suggests a pattern that is disconcerting and leads to the inducement and endorsement of differentiations between citizens. How would such polarization promote national unity?

Given the diversity and complexity of the Indian landscape, the only constitutionally valid common denominator is citizenship. This is the point at which fraternity can and should be prescribed and practised amongst equals.

Oommen, however, is not content with this and seeks 'an isomorphous model for India's socio-cultural reality.' He opines that it is 'only through the conflation of state and nation' can our Republic be considered a nation and that the expression 'India is a nation-in-the-making' be more relevant. He opines that cultural monoism and secularism are insufficient and, instead, 'the idea of

---

[17]Dr Ambedkar's Last Speech in The Constituent Assembly on Adoption of the Constitution (25 November 1949), https://tinyurl.com/mtxcrvwy. Accessed on 8 September 2025.

conceptualizing India as a multicultural polity is more amenable than a secular India.' The sheet anchor of this has to be citizenship.

There is a teaser towards the end in relation to Article 351 of the Constitution on the national language. Hindi is to be enriched by 'Hindustani' along with other languages in the Eighth Schedule; yet the latter does not figure in the list of the Eighth Schedule! Oommen instead suggests that 'India shall be a multicultural nation and not a nation-state having many identities,' and that eventually the preferable solution would lie in a confederation, USSA (United States of South Asia).

One is therefore bound to ask, could this be one way of giving shape to Bharat?

This article was originally published in The Hindu *on 12 May 2022, under the headline 'From Bharat to India'.*

Chapter 5

The Perils of Ideological Certitude

Trends, fashion or ideas float in all societies. When does a trend become an ideology? What motivates an individual to commit themselves to it?

An ideology is understood to mean a system of ideas that aspires to explain the world, and at times change it. Some call it the science of ideas aimed at serving people, ridding them of prejudice, preparing them for the sovereignty of a preferred idea.

This would seem to be obvious ever since humans indulged in deductive and inductive reasoning for sheer survival in daily life. This process matured with time and experience down the ages. When simple explanations were not discernable, the phenomena were attributed to superhuman or divine forces. Each of these sought justice between human beings living together. Hence, the dictum that justice is the first law of human institutions. Evidence of it is available in the ancient codes of China, Mesopotamia, India and elsewhere. Over time, these became religious codes and were duly sanctified. They all held out visions of an apogee of rectitude that humankind should endeavour to attain.

In all cases, the purpose was to regulate human behaviour in societies. The unstated premise in most societies was that the average member of a social group was too busy or simplistic or both, to discern the full meaning or implications and was, for the purposes of these laws, almost mindless in the sense of acting without a particular reason, ready and willing to observe the dicta and the accompanying suggestion of punishment in case of disobedience. Obedience was sought to become habitual.

QUEST FOR SOCIAL ORDER

The political atmospherics of the 19th and 20th centuries, particularly in Europe, sought to imbibe ideologies with their focus on change with greater meaning to the public. Hence, the assertion in Marx's *Theses on Feuerbach*: The philosophers have only interpreted the world in various ways; the point is to change it.

The 20th century had a surfeit of these, each addressing an intended audience ranging from local and regional to global and premised on an idealized social order. Each also portrayed a demonology premised on social class or ethnic specificity, from whose tyranny salvation was promised. Thus, communism, with its vision of a classless communist society promising to 'each according to his/her need', made sense to the disposed. Similarly, and apart from various versions of anarchism in European worker movements, national socialism in Germany and Italy tantalized its votaries with the focus on the nation and the fatherland. All of these found emulators in colonial lands in India, China and in some parts of western Asia. They were all characterized by what Eric Hobsbawm depicted as 'ruthless, brutal and command' versions of socialism[18].

FREEDOM, COMMUNAL IDEAS

In India, the germination of ideas of 'communal consciousness' (in cases with political overtones) on a societal scale alongside the urge for freedom from foreign rule surfaced in a segment of society in the closing decades of the 19th century. The efforts by

[18]Hobsbawm, Eric, *The Age of Extremes: A History of the World, 1914–1991*, Pantheon Publishers, New York, 1995, p. 498.

Mahatma Gandhi and his supporters were countered by many Hindus and Muslims, who deluded themselves into thinking that they belonged to separate 'nations'. The rest was done by the Mountbatten Plan in 1947, and the death and destruction that accompanied it.

The past three decades have witnessed the ease with which the Bharatiya Janata Party's political approach and tactics have made headway in the public mind. Electoral data in recent decades indicates the shift in its vote share, diligently and successfully built upon an exclusive identity in adversarial contrasts to what is dubbed non-Indic, meaning, principally, adherents of Zoroastrianism, Judaism, Christianity and Islam but politically focused on the latter two. Why and how has this order of priorities been put in place for a good segment of the electorate instead of the bread-and-butter governance issues? In state elections from 2014 to 2019, its vote share reached or crossed the 50 per cent mark in Haryana, Jharkhand, Karnataka, Delhi, etc. Political commentators attribute this and its subsequent spectacular success essentially to successful advocacy of majoritarianism.

AGENDA OF ARTIFICIAL LINES

Despite the dispersal of the minority population in most parts of India and the fact that in daily life all sections of people, majority and minorities, live in the same or adjacent neighbourhoods, and work together, artificial lines are sought to be drawn for laying the foundations of a majoritarian agenda by categorization of faiths on the basis of their places of origin. How far back in history can one go when confronted with M.S. Golwalkar's observation that 'Iran is nothing but the base of Aryabhumi' and part of 'grand picture of our motherland'?[19] So were the Aryans, and their faith

[19]Golwalkar, M.S., *Bunch of Thoughts*, Global Academic Publishers and Distributors, 2022.

and philosophy. Was it Indic or non-Indic?

It is considered convenient to recall Swami Vivekananda's letter of June 1898 in which he said, 'I am firmly persuaded that without the help of practical Islam theories of Vedantism, however fine and wonderful they may be, are entirely valueless to the vast mass of mankind,' adding that 'for our own motherland a junction of the two great systems, Hinduism and Islam—Vedanta brain and Islam body—is the only hope.'[20]

Also lost in the stated parameters of Hindutva is the constitutional imperative of fraternity.

The Hindutva agenda of viewing matters through the prism of faith has perhaps disrupted or weakened the post-Mandal equations and brought electoral gains; so has the intoxicating impact of the success of the Ram Mandir movement. It, however, cannot explain away the policy and its implementation challenges posed by the ongoing protests against the farm laws, the Citizenship (Amendment) Act, National Population Register, widespread unemployment and a host of other measures resulting in dire distress in most segments of society.

Does this 'ideological certitude' explain away the public distress and its widespread publicity within the country and in credible foreign media? Can it be attributed to a mindlessness of its supporters who are deluded by an uncritical ideological conviction? Would it reflect, public indoctrination notwithstanding, in the forthcoming state elections, and beyond it? Would the lord of Hindutva neither slumber nor sleep?

This article was originally published in The Hindu *on 29 October 2021, under the headline 'The perils of ideological certitude'.*

---

[20]Swami Vivekananda, https://tinyurl.com/mvax6b6k. Accessed on 2 September 2025.

Chapter 6

Nurturing Citizens in Social Studies

The list of jettisoned subjects is comprehensive; the apprehension that it is purposeful is unavoidable; the conclusion that a 'happening' has been converted into a 'penalty goal' is inescapable. These thoughts cross the mind while reading about the 2020 decision of the Ministry of Human Resource Development (MHRD) to exclude certain subjects from the list of topics of study[21] in the social science curriculum for Classes 9 to 12 with the objective of reducing by 30 per cent the 'load' while retaining 'core concepts'. The stated rationale of the move is the disruption caused by Covid-19 to the academic year. The exercise covers other subjects too, but the focus of this analysis is on the social sciences only for reasons that will become evident in this essay.

The argument for disruption and the resultant load is self-evident and valid. The phenomenon is universal and applies to all stages of education and to all lands across the globe. Not all have reacted the same way and pedagogues would argue that there could be more than one method of lightening the academic load that in any case predates the pandemic. Democratic societies the world over have developed methodologies of nurturing young citizens in

[21]Jebaraj, Priscilla, 'CBSE cuts syllabus by 30% for classes 9 to 12', *The Hindu*, 7 July 2020, https://tinyurl.com/ydywzvst. Accessed on 29 November 2025.

essential values and procedures and none have so far abandoned them on account of the pandemic.

SALIENT FEATURES OF CURRICULUM

The Central Board of Secondary Education (CBSE) on its website indicates nine salient features of the senior secondary school curriculum for Classes 11 and 12 for the years 2020–21. It mentions that the curriculum strives to 'provide ample scope for physical, intellectual and social development of students.'[22] The curriculum also strives to 'uphold Constitutional values such as Socialism, Secularism, Democracy, Republican character, Justice, Liberty, Equality, Fraternity, Human Dignity of Individual and Unity and Integrity of the Nation by encouraging value-based learning activities.'[23] With some abridgements, therefore, the features reiterate the values mentioned in the Preamble of the Constitution of India. Item 4 of the salient features says the curriculum strives to 'nurture Life-Skills by prescribing curricular and co-curricular activities to help improve self-esteem, empathy towards different cultures etc.'[24] There is, however, no mention of Fundamental Duties (Article 51A of the Constitution); of the duty 'to value and preserve the rich heritage of our composite culture' and of the duty 'to develop the scientific temper, humanism and the spirit of enquiry and reform.' The wording here is curious. Is 'different cultures' synonymous with our 'composite culture'? Is it an admission that ours is a land of 'different cultures'?

It would be argued in defence of abridgements that the CBSE curriculum for Classes 9 and 10 has identical wording for

[22]CBSE, *Senior Secondary School Curriculum 2020-21*, https://tinyurl.com/2satcwa7. Accessed on 18 September 2025.

[23]Ibid.

[24]Ibid.

items 3 and 4 and that the themes are therefore covered at an earlier stage of school education. This is to presume that levels of student comprehension between Classes 9 and 11 or 10 and 12 remain static and do not need upgradation either in teaching or in understanding.

BEING 'POLITICALLY CONSCIOUS'

Our system of democratic governance is based on the Constitution that prescribes universal adult suffrage with the voting age now being 18, after the 61st Amendment of 1988. It was then argued formally in parliament that 'the present-day youth are literate and enlightened and the lowering of the voting age would provide to the unrepresented youth of the country an opportunity to give vent to their feelings and help them become a part of the political process. The present-day youth are very much politically conscious. It is, therefore, proposed to reduce the voting age from 21 years to 18 years.'[25]

In other words, and since the general average school-leaving age after Class 12 is 16–17 years, this objective of being 'politically conscious' is to be attained suddenly at the age of 17 and without the benefit of formal instruction on fundamental principles of our polity. And, if this formal instruction on the principles of the Constitution is not available to the young person at that age, she or he has no option but to resort to informal knowledge acquired through hearsay and media or social media with all the tilt or prejudice of demagogy and propaganda that go with it. Would the young person exercising franchise for the first time then be an informed voter?

In this context, it is useful to examine the relevant portions

[25]The Constitution (Sixty-first Amendment) Act, 1988, https://tinyurl.com/4zf23jan. Accessed on 8 September 2025.

of the Draft National Education Policy 2019 with a message from the Minister of Human Resource Development. It has on page 96 a section on 'Development of Constitutional Values'. It states: 'The process and the content of education at all levels will also aim to develop Constitutional values in all students, and the capacities for their practice [...] Some of these Constitutional values are: democratic outlook and commitment to liberty and freedom; equality, justice, and fairness; embracing diversity, plurality, and inclusion; humanness and fraternal spirit; social responsibility and the spirit of service; ethics of integrity and honesty; scientific temper and commitment to rational and public dialogue; peace; social action through Constitutional means; unity and integrity of the nation, and a true rootedness and pride in India with a forward-looking spirit to continuously improve as a nation.'[26] The same document, on page 231, reiterates the objective of developing 'an understanding of our Constitutional values, and the disposition and capacities for their practice, amongst all their students.'[27] The other objectives mentioned in this section are diversity, plurality, humanness, fraternal spirit, scientific temper and commitment to rational dialogue.

FOCUS ON THE NEXT GENERATION

Will these virtues, constitutional values and capacities for their practice be developed without formal instruction? Would this necessarily be the best training for citizenship? Could the objective be to lessen the instruction in constitutional values and their impact on perceptions and practices of the next generation?

The BJP's Sankalp Patra for the 2019 general election mentions in several places the objective of good governance

---

[26]Draft National Education Policy 2019, p. 96, https://tinyurl.com/wdyaryvt. Accessed on 5 September 2025.

[27]Ibid., 231.

and of putting in place for it 'a framework of governance which will yield rich dividends over the next generation.'[28] This focus on the next generation requires good citizens who in turn need to be educated in good governance. This is precisely what the objective of the jettisoned items of the curriculum was intended to be. The proposed move of load-shedding goes counter to this and strikes at the target of training good citizens and teaching them civility. Would a sceptic be justified in suspecting that the objective may be to have a less literate young voter?

This article was originally published in The Hindu *on 13 July 2020 under the headline 'Nurturing citizens in social studies'.*

[28]Bharatiya Janata Party, *Sankalp Patra, Lok Sabha 2019*, p. 24, https://tinyurl.com/ysjec6ph. Accessed on 5 September 2025.

Chapter 7

Roll Back the Distrust

Sanity, said a line in an old movie, exists in every contract. It is so in every social compact that precedes the establishment of any society or social grouping. One is reminded of it by recent reports of expressions of hostility and downright hatred by a section of our people against another. Are these expressive of atavistic impulses of yore or are they generated by more recent trends seeking social hegemony premised on an imaginary past?

FOUNDATIONAL VALUES

The basic values of India's Constitution assert the principles of justice, equality and fraternity and are reiterated by all sections of social and political leadership. Yet, those who profess to be followers tend to forget these principles time and again.

In recent weeks, we have witnessed social debates and contestations, normal in a democracy, derail into aggressive assertions that typecast fellow citizens as enemies or undesirable creatures. The trend even finds its reflection in pronouncements of public figures and officials. Both have been prone to forget that even if a citizen is charged with an offence against the law or found to be guilty of it by the due process of law, he or she does not cease to be a citizen and stand deprived of rights and duties of citizenship. The conclusion is inescapable that the sole purpose of such typecasting is to find an excuse for an administrative failure and instead cast a slur, stigmatize and socially degrade a group of fellow citizens.

The trend is so pervasive that it finds expression in sections of our citizens living in foreign lands; it is so aggressive that it offends local sentiments and norms of behaviour; so alarming that it has invited reaction from otherwise friendly local hosts and compelled our authorities, belatedly, to state the official position at the highest level.

This ailment of the mind is being reflected in the discharge of normal duties by officials at different levels and is alarming enough to induce a group of 100 of our most eminent former civil servants to appeal, recently, to state chief ministers 'to instruct all public functionaries to be particularly vigilant to prevent social boycott of any community in the State and to ensure that all the entitlements including medical and hospital care, rations and financial assistance are available equally to all those in need.'[29]

APPROACH WORTH REITERATING

The plurality of our society and its diversity are an existential reality. The imperative of coexistence and tolerance has been accepted down the ages. Sages and society leaders have reiterated it time and again. We need only to recall Swami Vivekananda's advocacy of religious pluralism, his vision of India 'being the junction of two great systems, Hinduism and Islam, having a Vedantic brain and Islamic body.'[30]

This same approach in a more practical sense was reflected

[29]Constitutional Conduct Group, *Open Letter to the Prime Minister—Call for End to Politics of Hate*, 26 April 2022, https://tinyurl.com/5tbwxchm. Accessed on 24 September 2025.

[30]Vivekananda, Swami, 'Vedanata Brain and Islam Body—Only Hope for our Motherland', 10 June 1898, https://tinyurl.com/mvax6b6k. Accessed on 2 September 2025.

in the Inter-Communal Unity Appeal made in October 1923 by a group of Indians led by Lala Lajpat Rai, Mufti Kifayatullah, Swami Shraddhanand, Maulana Azad, Kasturba Gandhi and 95 others. All sections of our public need to be reminded of its pragmatic approach:

> If any individual or group of individuals belonging to any community commits an act of violence against, or attacks the person, property or honour of women or places of worship (mandir, mosque, church or gurdwara, etc) of his neighbour or townsman or helps those who indulge in such misdeeds, he is, from the religious point of view, guilty of a great sin; and that it is the duty of co-religionists of such offenders to stand up and resist such miscreants and to protect those who are so attacked.

Why can we not show the mirror in this shape to our professedly religion-minded public and urge it to follow in word and deed? The present approach of distrust is disquieting, resulting in resentment, and injection of suspicion and viciousness in social relations. It impacts adversely the promotion of fraternity. Is it serving any purpose, either of fighting the pandemic or of expediting the process of proceeding against those who may have transgressed the law? Alternatively, is it serving a political purpose?

History tells us that human relationships are fragile and need constant nursing; the same holds for societal relations. We have in our own times witnessed the fragmentation, even destruction, of societies elsewhere. Social peace is thus a pre-requisite for progress and development. Let sanity prevail. Let this be our motto.

This article was originally published in The Hindu *on 27 April 2020, under the headline 'Rollback the distrust, remember the core values'.*

Chapter 8

Media, Minorities and Majoritarianism

Over the years, at home and abroad, I have been broadly aware of this journal's claim to be 'the Muslim minority's representative voice' in our tumultuous society. Occasionally, it also echoes the emotional linkage of Muslims to the world of Islam beyond India.

October 22 is an anniversary, and anniversaries, of heart or mind, are events of joy for reciting virtues. Rarely but rarely do they enumerate shortfalls. Deviation from this pattern is frowned upon, perhaps rightly.

In this piece, therefore, I propose a wider foray. I plead forgiveness for transgressions. The subject of the intersection of media, minorities and majoritarianism interests me as a citizen. It may be of interest to you.

Years back, and in another context, a well-meaning friend had advised me to endeavour to abolish the distinction between majority and minority. 'Conceptually possible but less so in real life' was my diffident response. Yet, over the years these terms and some others contingent to them in their real and alleged import trouble me.

Some would recall that when the Constituent Assembly commenced its work in 1946, it had among others a sub-committee on minorities. In its final report in 1949 it voted against separate communal reservation. Congress leader Ajit Prasad Jain said on 22 November, 'None among us can be happy with a partition of the country, but nevertheless it must be admitted that this has smoothened our work of constitution-making. In particular the question of minorities which has been our headache and which thwarted all our efforts for the solution of national problems, has ceased to be live issue.'[31] Three days later, on 25 November, Sardar Patel said that 'in the interest of laying down "real and genuine foundations of a secular state in the country" nothing was better for the minorities than to trust the good sense and sense of fairness of the majority, and to place confidence in them. Like-wise the majority must think of what minorities felt.'[32] He expressed the fervent hope that in the long run, 'it would be in the interest of all to forget that there is anything like majority or minority in this country, and that in India there is only one community.'[33]

Three quarter of a century later, history makes its own judgement on intentions and reality.

THE GUIDING ETHOS

India is a democratic polity. Democracy is a form of government in which supreme power rests with people, exercised through direct or indirect elections. Experiences the world over have shown that the term expresses itself through adjectives that have multiplied with place and time and has led to pluralistic terms like people's democracy, guided democracy, ethnic democracy, direct democracy and parliamentary democracy.

---

[31]'Constituent Assembly Debates Volume 11, Draft Constitution (Contd.)', *Constitution of India*, https://tinyurl.com/3hhj6tp2. Accessed on 5 September 2025.

[32]Constituent Assembly Debates, 'Constituent Assembly Debates on 25 May, 1949, Part I', *Indian Kanoon*, https://tinyurl.com/y2ejumc7. Accessed on 5 September 2025.

[33]Ibid.

Democracy necessitates choice and the general practice is to make it the preferred option of the majority of electors. Its procedural niceties have always been a matter of critical importance.

We are a parliamentary democracy, with governance premised on the Constitution and a bill of rights that guarantees equality, justice and freedom of expression. It requires periodic elections. Freedom of expression through the media with all its diversity is guaranteed. The latter shows a good deal of variability across time and content. Studies in India and elsewhere show that this varies from non-recognition, ridicule and strict regulation to eventual expression and acceptance of diversity.

While legislature, executive and judiciary are accepted as the three pillars of democracy, the media in our times is considered its fourth pillar. Its origins go back to the days of our freedom struggle.

The rationale for journalism in a democracy is to inform, educate, guide and entertain. Each of these is a desired function, more so in modern societies whose size and numbers need means of communication other than direct face-to-face ones. This is sustained by law. The Supreme Court has held that 'the fundamental freedom under Article 19(1)(a) can be reasonably restricted only for the purposes mentioned in Articles 19(2) and the restriction must be justified on the anvil of necessity and not the quicksand of convenience or expediency. Open criticism of government policies and operations is not a ground for restricting expression. We must practise tolerance for the views of others. Intolerance is as much dangerous to democracy as to the person himself.

Democracy admittedly is rule by majority but its essential prerequisite is Rule of Law, defined by Dicey as (a) absolute supremacy of regular law, (b) equality before the law, and (c) access to justice and development of law by the judges on a case-by-case basis. This, as Prof. Upendra Baxi has argued, goes beyond a mere division of functions in modes of governance and incorporates the four core notions of rights, development, governance and justice. This approach has been upheld in judicial pronouncements and, as the Supreme Court said in the Dalmia Cement case in 1996, 'is a potent instrument of social justice to bring about equality in result.'

Yet, in a paper published in 2005, the late Goolam Vahanvati observed that 'the Rule of Law in this country is under serious threat,' adding that 'it would not be an overstatement if one concludes that each institution is destroying itself from within' and that 'there are cancerous developments eating into the fabric of each institution. If these trends are not arrested, they are bound to be destructive of the Indian state in the long run.'

How true is this of the media? To what extent is this being done? What happens when democracy is delinked from Rule of Law? In the words of an eminent critic, 'the role of the press in a democracy is different from that in a totalitarian state. Democracy is government by law, totalitarian state is government by authority; in the former decisions are arrived at by discussion, and in the latter by dictation; in the former the press acts as a check on authority, in the latter it is the handmaid of authority; in the former the press is necessarily to be free, as without free press there is no free discussion, in the latter the press supports authority.'

In the process, loaded terms have figured in the debate and assumed a high profile. They acquire specific meaning in the context of our times. I refer in particular to 'majority' and 'minority', 'majoritarian' and 'majoritarianism', 'self' and 'other', 'otherness' and 'hatred'. So also comes about the transition from democratic majority to populism, to authoritarianism, to ethnic majority and to the designation of fellow citizens as the 'Other'.

Studies have shown that democracies have been at times threatened by elected leaders who subvert the very process that brought them to power. 'The electoral road to breakdown is dangerously deceptive,' wrote Levitsky and Ziblatt in their 2018 book *How Democracies Die*. It opens the door to would-be authoritarians. They categorize key indicators of authoritarian behaviour as (i) weak commitment to democratic rules of the game, (ii) denial of the legitimacy of political opponents, (iii) toleration or encouragement of violence, and (iv) readiness to curtail civil liberties of opponents, including media.[34]

One consequence of authoritarian rule is majoritarianism, defined as the notion that the numerical majority of a population should have the final say in determining the outcome of a decision. It has pejorative connotations since it denotes a perceived superiority and a claim to arbitrary space and importance. It also requires 'a continuous demonstration of arbitrary power and submission of ideas, demands and identities that stand outside it.'[35]

This situation is aggravated manifold when majoritarianism is accompanied by an ideological superstructure designated as Hindutva or Hindu nationalism. It is described as an ideology advocating a movement seeking to establish the hegemony of Hindus and Hinduism within India. It is promoted through a sense of vulnerability in the public, facilitated through 'tentacular organisations' having strong affinities with the caste system. Badri Narayan Tiwari depicts it in *Republic of Hindutva*.

IN THE BUSINESS OF MEDIA

The socioeconomic changes of recent decades have highlighted a facet of the Fourth Estate that was less adequately appreciated earlier. The media now has an identifiable business and commercial persona and has been integrated in the market.

[34]Ziblatt, Daniel, and Steven Levitsky, *How Democracies Die*, Penguin Random House, 2019.

[35]Address by former Vice-President of India, Shri M. Hamid Ansari.

Today's media organizations are large business entities with thousands of employees and huge financial and other assets. While their primary professional duty is to their readership for keeping them informed and apprised of news, views and ideas, the commercial logic brings in new stakeholders in the shape of commercial interests.

These developments have brought into play a new set of considerations that guide the professional decisions of the press. The interplay of these conflicting demands is the subject of public debate. The phenomenal growth of the media industry, and intense competition within it, induces journalists and their supervisors to look as much at the top-line and bottom-line growth as at headlines and editorial content.

A perusal of the print and electronic media today is suggestive of the tilting balance between news and advertising content and the fading distinction between editorials and advertorials. The emergence of the Internet and 24×7 television as well as social media reporting have put additional pressure on the print media.

The phenomenon is global and has been commented upon. At the other end of the spectrum, we have the development of grassroots journalism, the subject of an interesting study by Dan Gillmor two years before Twitter was born. He opined that 'tomorrow's news reporting and production will be more of a conversation or a seminar.'[36]

The paradigm shift in the production, transmission and consumption of media products has major consequences for three constituencies: journalists, newsmakers and the audience. The convergence between news media, entertainment and social media has eroded the demarcation between journalism, public relations, advertising and entertainment. This has created new

---

[36]Gillmor, Dan, 'We the Media: Grassroots Journalism by the People, for the People', *O'Reilly Media*, California, 2004, p. 9, https://tinyurl.com/yc7tszt3. Accessed on 5 September 2025.

ethical dilemmas that lie at the core of many issues of debate today and pose questions.

Has the media upheld the social and political compact that our people gave it through our Constitution?

The deteriorating situation in the media is reflected in the World Press Freedom Index 2023 that ranks India 161 out of 180 countries; this was 150 in 2022[37] and 140 in 2014[38]. The position improved to 159 in 2024 but this was courtesy of other countries falling on the index.[39] A democratic backslide in media's role as the fourth estate is the end result.

What then is the meaning of democratic majority? How is it to be distinguished from ochlocracy or the tyranny of the majority? If majority is separated from the rule of law, how can its political and ethical rectitude be ensured? And, how does all this affect the minorities?

MODERNITY AND MINORITIES

Modern states are non-homogenous entities composed mostly of diverse elements in ethnic, linguistic and religious terms. They have ethnic minorities. A minority in the territory of a state means it is not the majority. The makers of the Constitution of India accepted as a living reality the diversity of India in religious and linguistic terms. They also accepted the plural ethos.

The Indian polity has the most elaborate set of identities

---

[37] *The Hindu* Bureau, 'India Slips in World Press Freedom Index, Ranks 161 out of 180 countries', *The Hindu*, 4 May 2023, https://tinyurl.com/3t2cdex4.Accessed on 5 September 2025.

[38] Agencies, 'In World Press Freedom Index, India ranks 140th', *The Times of India*, 13 February 2014, https://tinyurl.com/4b6j4sse. Accessed on 5 September 2025.

[39] Lakshman, Sriram, 'India Press Freedom Score Falls, says Reporters sans Frontiers', *The Hindu*, 3 May 2024, https://tinyurl.com/4e8dxjc7. Accessed on 5 September 2025.

based on class, religion, gender, caste, region and language. Our linguistic diversity is reflected in the currency notes written in seventeen different scripts. India thus should be viewed as a multicultural polity rather than merely as secular.

As per the 2001 Census data, religious minorities constitute 18.4 per cent of India's population.[40] That percentage has marginally increased to 19.3 per cent in the 2011 Census data.[41] Thus, every fifth or sixth Indian has a religious minority affiliation. Articles 25 to 30 of the Constitution guarantee the freedom of religion and of cultural and educational rights of all sections of citizens, and circumscribe the tyranny of majority in any one sense.

What do religious minorities seek from the state and the social apparatus?

In specific terms, they seek (i) identity and security, (ii) education and empowerment, (iii) equitable share in the largesse of the state, and (iv) a fair share in decision-making. Each of this is a right and has to be dispensed without discrimination. This is true in good measure of the Muslims who constitute 14.2 per cent of the population and now number over 200 million.[42] Yet, as an editorial comment opined recently, 'India is witnessing the progressive normalization of minority baiting.' The official claim however is that 'we are a democratic polity with strong commitment to rule of law.'

The happenings of 1947 and the events preceding and following it cast a shadow of physical and psychological insecurity among Indian Muslims who were made to carry its burden unfairly.

---

[40]National Commission for Minorities, https://tinyurl.com/m9s5zyn5. Accessed on 5 September 2025.

[41]Ministry of Minority Affairs, https://tinyurl.com/2sd9kekr. Accessed on 5 September 2025.

[42]Kramer, Stephanie, 'Key Findings about the Religious Composition of India', *Pew Research Center*, 21 September 2021, https://tinyurl.com/5n6ad9mj. Accessed on 5 September 2025.

The process of recovery from that trauma has been gradual and uneven, and at times painful. They have hesitatingly sought to tend to their wounds, face the challenges and seek to develop response patterns. Success has been achieved in some measure; much more, however, needs to be done.

In recent decades, work has also been initiated to delineate the contours of the problem. The Sachar Committee Report of 2006 did this officially. It laid to rest the political untruth in some quarters about the Muslim condition and demonstrated that on most socioeconomic indicators, they were on the margins of structures of political, economic and social relevance, and their average condition was comparable to or even worse than the country's acknowledged historically most backward communities, the Scheduled Castes and Scheduled Tribes. It specified the development deficits of the majority of Muslims in regard to education, livelihood and access to public services and the employment market across the states.

Pursuant to the Sachar Report, Expert Group reports were prepared in 2008 on the need to develop a Diversity Index and establish an Equal Opportunity Commission. Taken together, these and other studies bring forth sufficient evidence to substantiate the view that 'inequality traps keep the marginalized excluded and work in favour of the dominant groups in society.'[43]

Subsequently, the Kundu Report of September 2014, commissioned to evaluate the implementation of decisions taken pursuant to Sachar recommendations, concluded that though 'a start has been made, yet serious bottlenecks remain.' It observed that 'available financial resources and physical targets have been meagre in relation to the deprived minorities, especially Muslims, and for some of the schemes this meagre amount has not been

[43]Sachar, Rajindar, 'Social, Economic and Educational Status of the Muslim Community of India', Prime Minister's High Level Committee Cabinet Secretariat, https://tinyurl.com/2bf9scnv. Accessed on 5 September 2025.

fully utilized.' It makes specific recommendations to remedy these. It asserted that 'development for the Muslim minority must be built on a bedrock of a sense of security.'[44]

This, however, is not happening.

It is evident from these reports that the principal problems confronting India's Muslims relate in greater degree to the shortfalls that affect other minorities. Each of these is a right of the citizen. The shortcomings in regard to each have been analysed threadbare. Identity is unquestionably linked to ordinary expressions of faith and of language that is often transgressed socially; both need to be protected within the legal framework.

The challenge before us today is to develop strategies and methodologies to address them.

Instances of breach of security at individual or group level continue to occur with disturbing frequency. Most reveal a failure of the state apparatus to respond in a timely manner, compounded by failure of media houses that often 'dictate a majoritarian mindset'. A good instance of it is the report, entitled *Delhi's Agony*, on the communal violence in Delhi in February 2020 and its section subtitled the 'Aftermath'.

Civil society reports on violence elsewhere, and court observations relating to them, like the Punjab & Haryana High Court ruling recently in August, suggest a disturbing pattern of studied neglect by local or state administrations.

The default by the state or its agents in terms of deprivation, exclusion and discrimination (including failure to provide security) is to be corrected by the state; this needs to be done at the earliest and appropriate instruments developed for it. Political sagacity, the imperative of social peace, and public opinion play an important role in it. Experience shows that the corrective has to

---

[44]Post Sachar Evaluation Committee, https://tinyurl.com/4khyu3h7. Accessed on 5 September 2025.

be at both the policy and the implementation levels; the latter, in particular, necessitates mechanisms to ensure active cooperation of the state governments whose response is often tardy.

One aspect of the Delhi Report is its section on 'Hate as State Project' and its observation that: 'India is witnessing a carefully crafted phenomenon. Hate as State Project, concertedly unleashed against the most marginalized sections of our population.' Since both hate and polarization need vehicles for dissemination, the 24-hour news television and sections of social media provide the platform for it. Instances of it also surfaced in the first phase of Covid.

Hate is a toxic tonic. It is, regrettably, becoming part of normal discourse and is not being discouraged. Hate crimes convey a message to targeted communities that they are unwelcome and unsafe, impacting the collective sense of security and well-being. It has been suggested that it necessitates a collective effort involving legislative reforms, sensitization campaigns, community policing and youth engagement.

The official objective of *sab ka saath sab ka vikas* is commendable; a pre-requisite for it however is affirmative action to ensure a common starting point and an ability in all to walk at the required pace. This ability has to be developed through individual, social and governmental initiatives that fructify on the ground. Programmes have been made in abundance; the need of the hour is their implementation.

The experience of several decades makes it evident that meaningful correctives would not originate from official agencies and programmes, and that they have to emanate at individual, group and community levels, and cover both genders. They have to be realistic, grounded in the situation, and devoid of unrealism and nostalgia.

What are these correctives? In the first place, precedence has to be given to self-reliance. Alongside, and looking at what has been done by other minority communities in India and elsewhere, organized community effort has to be promoted as an imperative and in an atmosphere of self-help.

Autonomously, a beginning has to be made with education to fill the gap in levels for both boys and girls as well as for adults. Details of both, including dropout rates, have been quantified and I had mentioned and observed that the equality bestowed by faith was diluted or denied by tradition and practice. Particularly disturbing were details of educational levels of girls and the participation of Muslim women in the workforce.

Associated with it is the imperative of inducing young people—men and women—to diligently acquire skills in different professions, notwithstanding the actual or alleged effort in some quarters at explicit discrimination. The effort in all cases has to be on quality since, in the final analysis, such efforts fail when confronted by quality differentiation. In the same vein, independent efforts directed at initiation of small enterprises would bring forth both employment and self-reliance on the pattern of what is being done by other minority communities.

These requirements have to be quantified for better performance.

FUTURE STEPS

The population of India is dispersed, has no legal restrictions on locations of residence, and is broadly though not specifically integrated. It adheres mostly to being plural and democratic and is devoted to principles of pluralism. Departures from it, noticeable of late, is disturbing.

Assimilation with fellow citizens is not a legal requirement but does happen sporadically. This is highly desirable and needs to be strengthened and accelerated. Hence the need for emotional integration and for overcoming problems posed by it from time to time. This effort to assimilate without loss or dilution of identity or identity markers has to be made in the context of Indian conditions and the uniqueness of its three dimensions: plural, secular and democratic. It would be always challenging.

An attempt to implement it can only be made in the context of the Constitution of India and its prescription, and in the principles of Equality and Fraternity enunciated in the Preamble.

Experience tells us that seeking special facilities in the shape of reservations will not be fruitful and the quest for Scheduled Caste status for relevant segments of Muslims and Christians, however justified, would not be conceded politically. A more productive option may be to focus on citizenship rights and their equal dispensation.

Quantifying the corrective and the requirements of the present-day situation is one aspect of this. We have to go beyond it and induce our fellow citizens—through the power of our words—to take an active part in bringing about the required change.

This was originally an address on 'Media and Minorities' organized by Radiance Viewsweekly *on 23 October 2023.*

Chapter 9

Power and Diplomacy

Dr Zorawar Daulet Singh's study is of Indian foreign policies (yes, in plural) during the Cold War as an international system that extended from 1945 to 1989. He has developed an analytical framework to examine these in two phases: 'peace makers' and 'security seekers'. The case studies are illustrative.

Odd Arne Westad, in his seminal history of the Cold War, asserts that 'if there was a Cold War wild card it was India.' Nehru, he concludes, was repelled by it as an international system and 'was fiercely opposed to the concept of power blocs.'[45] This came out vividly during Nehru's discussions with President Truman in 1950 and the latter's remark that 'Nehru has sold us down the Hudson' and his attitude has been 'responsible for us losing the war in Korea.' No other Indian leader has earned such a left-handed compliment in Washington, though another was the subject of remarks that, to quote Westad again, 'oozed racism and misogyny.'[46]

Dr Singh's *Power and Diplomacy: India's Foreign Policies during the Cold War* diligently traces this and other crises of that period in Nehru's concept of India as peacemaker with a preference for ethical statecraft relying on persuasion rather than coercion. He brings out, in Chapter 2, contradictory elements between the

---

[45]Westad, Odd Arne, *The Cold War: A World History*, Penguin Random House, Ireland, 2018.

[46]Ibid.

ideals and principles of a policy of peace as well as the imperatives of a crisis in the immediate neighbourhood. Some of those debates have a contemporary resonance.

A complex judgement on Nehru is unavoidable. His focus was on avoidance of war and on furtherance of cooperation to India's benefit and retention of policy choices in an age when power bloc politics tended to predetermine them. He sought to accommodate this approach to the imperatives of power politics that were thrust upon him. The end product was a visionary who also possessed the requisite traits of *realpolitik*. Nuances are discernable; a case in point is Churchill's telegram of thanks (1 July 1953) 'for the help you gave us over Egypt and Israel.[47]' At the same time, while describing British action over Suez as a 'worse case of aggression', he advised President Nasser after the war to refrain from deporting British and French nationals and persons of Jewish origin from Egypt—an advice that was not taken.

Indira Gandhi confronted a different set of situations. *Power and Diplomacy*'s analysis of the Vietnam War brings out the conflicting forces in play. Zorawar Daulet Singh concludes that it gave 'credence to a credible independent posture that kept India in the game and prevented it from losing strategic support from either of the superpowers.'

New archival material adds greatly to the book's analysis of the Bangladesh crisis and the policy debate in New Delhi. It shows how a demand for regional autonomy and its reflection in an electoral verdict was turned by a neighbour into tactical gain and wider strategic benefit. The critical decisions were taken early. The Pakistani Army crackdown on 25 March 1971 was followed by Indira Gandhi's speech in Parliament on 31 March and early diplomatic initiatives directed at foreign powers.

---

[47]Gopal, Sarvepalli, *Jawaharlal Nehru: A Biography, Volume 2,* Oxford University Press, Delhi, 1979, p. 170.

The effort was to define the crisis in terms of denial of democracy and human rights, and its resultant implications for India through the massive inflow of refugees. The process involved seeking the support of one great power to counteract the possibility of a third-party intervention in favour of Pakistan. This was undertaken successfully and the author's conclusion is that Indira Gandhi was motivated primarily by realpolitik reasons aimed at giving India a free hand in the neighbourhood.

I conclude with one last observation. Foreign policy anywhere is about promotion of national interest which includes threats to national security and perceptions of it in domestic politics. The latter necessitates a complex exercise. The annual reports of the ministries of defence and external affairs focus primarily on external threats. The Home Ministry's report, on the other hand, has a typology of four threats to security: (a) terrorism in the hinterland, (b) left-wing extremism, (c) cross-border threats principally in J&K, and (d) insurgency in northeast. Most of these are domestic, are of a sociopolitical nature, and their persistence sheds light on grievances relating to governance in its local, regional and federal manifestations.

> The Indian statecraft during the Cold War forms an essential part of its strategic culture and Indian security thinking and behavior in the emerging multipolar world will more likely than not have elements of the past embedded in it.[48]

This was originally an address at the launch of the book Power and Diplomacy: India's Foreign Policies during the Cold War, *authored by Zorawar Daulet Singh, on 5 April 2019 at India International Centre, New Delhi.*

---

[48]Singh, Zorawar Daulet, *Power and Diplomacy: India's Foreign Policies during the Cold War*, Oxford University Press, Delhi, 2018, p. 361.

Chapter 10

In the Name of Our Mother

Khwaja Ahmad Abbas played an integral and substantial role in shaping the national consciousness in his age, in another era, in an idiom when being open-minded and progressive was perhaps relatively easier. He had taken to heart Jawaharlal Nehru's advice to 'live dangerously' and felt free enough to practise it in his work.

By his own description, Abbas was 'a communicator of ideas', an advocate of causes, not an adherent of ideological conformity. This is reflected in his writings over decades and was explicitly brought out in the piece *Communism and I.*

Abbas was a discriminating Nehruvian, as is evident from his three essays entitled *My Long Love Affairs.* He subscribed to Nehru's faith in the basic values of the Constitution of India summed up as democracy, religious tolerance, economic development and cultural pluralism.

His power of imagination is well portrayed in an essay on what he called 'the most popular slogan of the Indian national movement' and on what encounters with Gandhi did to ordinary people. It is titled *Five Faces of Mother India* and is devoted to the concept of a collective Mother India as depicted by five humble unknown women 'who, between them summed up and symbolised after their encounter with Gandhi and his ways the eternal grace, the life-giving maternal devotion, the earthly wisdom and abiding faith that one likes to associate with the concept of Supreme Mother.'[49]

[49] Abbas, Khwaja Ahmad, *Five Faces of Mother India,* Pratham Books, Delhi, 2019.

The first of these, *Khaddar Shroud*, is a childhood memory of the wizened face of an old woman and the impact on her life after listening to Gandhi in Panipat. The second, *The Defeat of Manu*, raises and answers the question: does Mother India who is the Mother Supreme of all the people of this country also believe in Manu's divisions and castes or would she defy the ancient social code? The third, *Flowers in Her Hair, Dust on Her Feet*, depicts how a South Indian Brahmin family overcomes their traditional, orthodox ways. The fourth, *The Refugee*, shows how Mother India in the shape of the intensely human heart of a refugee woman from Rawalpindi has neither anger nor hatred but only memories. The fifth, *A Bit of India in Pakistan!*, is the author's own mother who migrated to Karachi but from her death bed sought permission to return to die in India. Permission to resume her citizenship was given but death preceded her journey. 'She in a Karachi graveyard, but her soul, her memory, the ideal of her life, are with us in India. And six feet of earth in Pakistan will forever be Indian soil—for buried in it is my mother, who also was Mother India.'[50]

PAST FOR FUTURE LESSONS

Seven decades later, the consciousness of yore is under assault. We have to ask individually, and as a people, how committed are we to these in actual practice? If not, where and why did we fail? Do we have alternatives for reaching the common good?

Let me dwell on the optimistic. The last two months have shown a remarkable aspect of the Indian civic character, namely, the capacity of the citizen body to go beyond formal structures of opinion of groups and political parties and instead come together spontaneously to raise their voice for a good cause in a

[50]Ibid.

very Gandhian way—of peaceful agitation. What are passionately and prominently on display are the *Tiranga*, the Preamble of the Constitution and the singing of the National Anthem.

The flag symbolizes the unity under its banner of *We the People of India*. So do the National Anthem, and the principles and values inscribed in the Preamble. The latter have a sequential order that is critical to understanding them: Justice, Liberty, Equality and Fraternity. Thus, fraternity cannot be achieved without dispensing justice, liberty and equality to the citizens.

How would have Khwaja Ahmad Abbas reacted to this form of public action? How would he, the journalist, the filmmaker and the story writer, respond to the challenge of interpreting this form of expression of dissent?

My guess is that he would be ingeniously creative, as inventive as the newly born sources of hope scattered around the four corners of our land, nameless but not faceless, assertive in their claiming of constitutional rights, in rejection of charity, boldly facing the edifice put in place by their own exercise of franchise but not afraid of confronting the Leviathan, the monster that goes by the name of the present-day Indian state and its antics of infinite cleverness in deforming revered institutions and endowing their functioning with an unprecedented elasticity of time in initiating the processes of accountability and restoring public trust.

Amidst last week's scenes of doom and gloom, I happened to re-read an old piece, pre-1947, written by Khwaja Ahmad Abbas: *Who Killed India*. It reproduced a passage from the column he penned every week for the Bombay weekly *Blitz:*

> India was killed and stabbed in the heart, by every Hindu who killed a Muslim, by every Muslim who killed a Hindu, by every Hindu or Muslim who committed or abetted or connived at arson, rape and murder during the recent (and earlier) communal riots.

> That an imperialist power planned the dismemberment of our country in the very hour of our freedom is not surprising. The wonder, and the tragedy, is that India should have been killed by the children of India.[51]

Do we learn nothing? Must we continue to repeat our own past?

Na samjhoge to mit jaaoge ai Hindostan walon...[52]

This was originally an address at a seminar organized by Khwaja Ahmad Abbas Memorial Trust at India International Centre, New Delhi, on 29 February 2020.

[51]Abbas, Khwaja Ahmad, 'Who Killed India? (Selected Writings of K.A. Abbas)', *Sahapedia*, https://tinyurl.com/ycyy773e. Accessed on 5 September 2025.

[52]Iqbal, Allama, *Paiman-e-gazal-avval, Volume 1*, National Book Foundation, Karachi, 2008, p. 274.

Chapter 11

The Great Pertinence of Gandhi to India

A thesaurus would dwell on the difference between 'relevance' and 'pertinence' with the former implying a general and the latter suggesting a more specific impact. Thus, while the progress of our freedom movement was part of a wider process, the impact of Gandhi's personality was critical in imparting it shape and direction. The manner of its impact on the Indian mind is worthy of careful study.

So, who was Gandhi? Why was he relevant to his contemporaries? How do we evaluate his bequest to our times?

Allow me to recall a famous passage:

> This little man of poor physique had something of steel in him, something rock-like which did not yield to physical powers, however great they might be. And in spite of his unimpressive features, his loin cloth and bare body, there was a royalty and kingliness in him which compelled a willing obedience from others. Consciously and deliberately meek and humble, yet he was full of power and authority, and he knew it, and at times he was imperious enough, issuing commands which had to be obeyed [...] Whether his audience consisted of one person or a thousand, the charm and magnetism of the man passed on to it, and each one had a feeling of communion with the speaker [...] one of the most remarkable things about Gandhi ji was, and is, his

> capacity to win over, or at least, to disarm his opponents [...] Having found an inner peace, he radiated it to others and marched through life's tortuous ways with firm and undaunted steps.[53]

So described by Jawaharlal Nehru was the man who held India and Indians spellbound in his lifetime, and does so to this day.

A biography cannot be compressed in an essay and so my effort today would be to focus on the formative period of the Gandhian ideology and methodology and the final outcome because these left an imprint on the Indian mind and shaped the approach of ordinary Indians.

A MAN OF HIS OWN KIND

After his studies in the UK and his sojourn in South Africa in the course of which some of his techniques of passive resistance were initiated, Gandhi returned to India 'a mature idealist and political mobiliser'. The political establishment in South Africa heaved a sigh of relief: 'The saint has left our shore', wrote Smut, 'I sincerely hope for ever.'[54] He was, in some matters, influenced by both Gokhale and Tilak. These early years were critical to the shaping of his mind and of the principles and practice of *Brahmachariya*, *Satyagraha*, *Ahimsa*. He studied other religions, found virtues in all of them, and scrupulously adhered to his self-definition of a Sanatani Hindu (given later in *Young India* on 12 October 1921). Elsewhere, he described his language as 'aphoristic; it lacks precision. It is therefore open to several interpretations.' He wrote in *Young India* that 'I am not anti-British [...] but I am

---

[53]Gandhi Center, 'Jewarhalal Nehru', Gandhi Memorial Center, 19 July 2020, https://tinyurl.com/mu7pj576. Accessed on 24 September 2025.

[54]Judd, Denis, *Empire: The British Imperial Experience From 1765 To The Present*, I.B. Tauris, 2012.

anti-untruth, anti-humbug and anti-injustice [...] No Indian has cooperated with the British Government more than I have...'[55]

His political thoughts were first expressed in *Hind Swaraj* published in 1908. It asserted self-rule, also a rejection of modernity. The book is fascinating to read, more difficult to implement as a guide to political action since, as Gandhi himself admitted, 'politics encircles us today on the coil of a snake.'[56]

Gandhi's earliest involvement in India was in the Champaran Satyagraha of 1917 where he adopted the approach of civil disobedience movement resulting in a committee set up by the government and proposals that were acceptable to the agitating cultivators. A second movement was the Kheda Satyagraha in 1917–18 in Kheda in Gujarat seeking remission of taxes due to crop failure. Here too a response was forthcoming from the government.

Champaran and Kaira, and the industrial dispute in Ahmadabad, were first instances of Satyagraha in practice in India. Both hammered home the lesson that Satyagraha could be used 'in virtually any situation of conflict, by literate and illiterate. It was a weapon for all seasons and, in Gandhi's hands, directed by his personal ideology, it gave him the edge over conventional politicians with their techniques of petitions, public speeches and debates, which were more suitable for the educated.'[57] Equally critical was the Rowlatt Satyagraha that 'radically altered Gandhi's standing with the government [...] and showed Gandhi as an all-India leader of immense potential.'[58]

---

[55]Gandhi, Mahatma, *The Collected Works of Mahatma Gandhi*, Valji Govindji Desai (trans.), S. Ganeshan Publisher, Madras, p. 523.

[56]Thus Spake Gandhi, https://tinyurl.com/3nv9v739. Accessed on 24 September 2025.

[57]Occasional Publication 109, 'The Great Pertinence of Gandhi to India in the 75th Year of Its Independence', India International Centre, https://tinyurl.com/4nsw89s3. Accessed on 24 September 2025.

[58]Brown, Judith M., *Gandhi's Rise to Power: Indian Politics 1915–1922*, Cambridge University Press, India, 1972, p. 106.

His tactics had an impact, and so did his general appearance. An intelligence report in May 1920 assessed that 'the association of Gandhi with any movement is a great asset because his name is one to conjure with among the ignorant masses.'[59] A report by the Governor of Madras to the Viceroy in April 1921 said 'it is amazing what an influence this man is gathering [...] There is no doubt that Gandhi has got a tremendous hold on the public imagination.'[60]

Gandhi supported the Khilafat Movement for multiple reasons: a demand for fulfilment of British pledges given to the Muslims, his own sense of moral responsibility, and to secure Hindu-Muslim friendship. He explained it in his own words in May 1920: 'If I had not joined the Khilafat movement, I think, I would have lost everything. In joining it I have followed what I especially regard as my dharma. I am trying to show through this movement the real nature of non-violence. I am uniting Hindus and Muslims. The Khilafat movement is a great churning of the sea of India. Why should we be concerned with what it will produce? All that we should consider is whether the movement itself is pure and worthy.'[61]

Gandhi considered his participation in the Amritsar session of the Indian National Congress (1919) his 'real entrance into Congress politics.' After the Jallianwala Bagh Massacre, he took an active part in the collection of funds for the Memorial to that massacre and also for the redrafting of the Congress Rules that resulted in a unanimous report. It sought to make the Congress pyramidal in structure, more representative and more functional between annual sessions. This was a key innovation that allowed regional committees greater freedom to participate in proceedings.

---

[59]Ibid.

[60]Ibid.

[61]'Letter to Maganlal Gandhi', https://tinyurl.com/2s49nppw. Accessed on 29 September 2025.

Gradualism was the essence of his approach. 'My life, through insistence on truth, has taught me the beauty of compromise.'[62] When, in the 1921 session of the Indian National Congress, Maulana Hasrat Mohani (who coined the slogan *Inquilab zindabad)* proposed a resolution seeking 'Swaraj or complete independence free from all foreign control' to be the objective of Congress, Gandhi demurred: 'let us not go into waters whose depth we do not know' and suggested other priorities[63].

And yet, there was clarity of vision in his perceptions. In a letter to Dr B.C. Roy in May 1928, he wrote: 'I am bidding my time and you will find me leading the country in the field of politics when the country is ready. I have no false modesty about me. I am undoubtedly a politician in my own way, and I have a scheme for the country's freedom. But my time is not yet and may never come to me in this life.'[64]

TURNING POINTS

Any study of the intrinsic principles of Gandhi's thinking, and of his major political interventions, would show the extent to which the two were intertwined. His autobiography records his reading of Ruskin's *Unto This Last* and his own remark that it 'captured me and made me transform my life.'[65]

Gandhi's elaboration of some of his practices was unique. He defined passive resistance as 'a method of securing rights by personal suffering and the reverse of resistance by arms.'

[62]'My Inconsistencies', https://tinyurl.com/2hyzjks8. Accessed on 29 September 2025.

[63]Siddiqi, Nafees Ahmad, *Hasrat Mohani aur Inqilab-e Aazadi*, Oxford University Press, Karachi, 2004, pp. 220–228.

[64]Brown, Judith, *Gandhi: Prisoner of Hope*, Yale University Press, 1991, p. 213.

[65]Mehta, Ashish, 'On John Ruskin's 200th birth anniversary, a look at how his seminal work *Unto This Last* inspired Mahatma Gandhi', *MKGandhi.org*, https://tinyurl.com/4at3ubtv. Accessed on 29 September 2025.

It requires fearlessness. He chose themes for agitations that appealed to the poorest and the simplest. An Urdu poet summed up his style:

Lashkar-e-Gandhi ko hathyaron ki hajat kuch nahin
Han magar be-intiha sabr-o-qanaat chahiye[66]

(The army of Gandhi does not need any weapons
Yes, but it does need limitless contentment and patience.)

His personality, lifestyle and simplicity, and the idiom of his communication, caught the imagination of the public. His ashram in Ahmadabad added to the transmission of being regarded a Mahatma. 'It is the fakir's dress that has broken down all barriers,' wrote Abbas Tyabji, a former chief justice of Baroda[67]. Jawaharlal Nehru wrote that the movement absorbed him so wholly that he 'gave up all other associations and contacts.' Through 1921, the tension between the Congress and the Government mounted; first the Ali Brothers and then many Congress leaders were arrested on charges of sedition.

The Turkish novelist and feminist Halide Adib spent the early months of 1935 in India, some of it with Gandhi, and recorded her impressions in *Inside India* first published in 1937. One chapter of the book recorded his 'Eleven Vows' and his manifold activities aimed 'to build the Indian society from the bottom to the top and focuses on the abolition of Untouchability, the regeneration of the village as a unit of Indian society, and achievement of communal unity.'[68]

---

[66]Occasional Publication 109, 'The Great Pertinence of Gandhi to India in the 75th Year of Its Independence', India International Centre, https://tinyurl.com/4nsw89s3. Accessed on 24 September 2025.

[67]Kazmi, S.M.A., 'Abbas Tyabbji- the Grand Old Man of Gujarat, a Forgotten Prominent Freedom Fighter', *The Northern Gazette*, 3 March 2024, https://tinyurl.com/mp87ucnt. Accessed on 24 September 2025.

[68]Halide, Edib, *Inside India*, Unwin Brothers Ltd., Woking, Great Britain, 1937, p. 43.

Gandhi's major campaigns against the British rule were the Non-Cooperation Movement of the 1920s, the civil disobedience movements of the 1930s of which the Salt Satyagraha was the highlight, and the Quit India Movement of the 1940s.

'How did one coax an aggrieved yet disarmed, heterogeneous and divided populace to wage an assault on a powerful empire?' Tagore posed the question to Gandhi on 18 January 1930, and the latter said, 'I am furiously thinking night and day.' In the middle of February, 'the intuition came to him like a flash: the assault should be over salt. Gandhi pictured a march to the sea by his ashramite army, with himself at the head. It had another virtue: all could jointly oppose it, Hindus and Muslims, peasants and the landless. Also known as the Dandi March, it attracted a great many people including Jawaharlal Nehru and Sarojini Naidu, resulted in violence by the police and the arrest of 60,000 people.'[69]

The Non-Cooperation Movement in 1920–22 was organized to induce the British Government in India to grant self-rule or *swaraj* to India. His speech in Madras on 12 August 1920 spelt out the essence of the doctrine of non-cooperation. It was Gandhi's first organized act of large-scale civil disobedience. It gathered strength by joining forces with the Khilafat Movement launched by the Muslims of India against the British breach of promises made with regard to Ottoman Turkey. For a variety of reasons, it had a limited life span and the violence in the village of Chauri Chaura made Gandhi call it off, much to the 'disappointment and anger' of Nehru. Nevertheless, it marked the transition from a middle class to a mass basis.

A spell of imprisonment followed by the Gandhi-Irwin Pact created space for political negotiations. Gandhi attended the

---

[69]Occasional Publication 109, 'The Great Pertinence of Gandhi to India in the 75th Year of Its Independence', India International Centre, https://tinyurl.com/4nsw89s3. Accessed on 24 September 2025.

Second Round Table Conference in London but was imprisoned on return. The Gandhi-Ambedkar talks resolved the question of separate electorate for the Dalits. On the proposed negotiations leading to the Government of India Act, 1935, Gandhi's view was that it was an act of the sword, not of goodwill. He had earlier resigned from the primary membership of the Congress and left the decision-making to the Congress leadership that accepted the clarifications given by the Viceroy. In the elections that followed, the Congress won overwhelmingly.

The Quit India Movement of August 1942 that demanded an end to British rule in India was launched by Gandhi with a speech whose focus was on Ahimsa: 'The draft Resolution of the Working Committee is based on Ahimsa […] Ours is not a drive for power, but purely a non-violent fight for India's independence […] The Congress is unconcerned as to who will rule when freedom is attained. The power when it comes will belong to the people of India…'[70]

He called for an 'orderly British withdrawal' from India and described the promised withdrawal after the war as 'a post-dated cheque on a crashing bank'. This was unacceptable to the British who imprisoned the entire Congress leadership. It is of course another matter that the Quit India Movement was opposed by segments of Indian opinion including the Muslim League, the Hindu Mahasabha, the CPI and the Indian states who felt a fight against the Axis powers should take precedence.

The modest dwelling in Wardha to which Gandhi often withdrew had an aberration: a telephone. It was explained to me that this was at the insistence of the British authorities!

When political negotiations were resumed after the war and the Partition Plan was presented, Gandhi told Dr Rajendra Prasad,

---

[70]'The "Quit India" Resolution', https://tinyurl.com/yv2h9pu3. Accessed on 29 September 2025.

'I can see only evil in the plan.' This was expressed candidly in the latter's Introduction to Pyare Lal Nayar's book *Gandhi: Going to Wipe their Tears*:

> Gandhiji was uncompromisingly opposed to the Partition of India, which he called her vivisection [...] Based on a wrong theory and brought about by such questionable means, it would do irretrievable harm to both Hindus and Muslims—in India and in Pakistan. But he left it to the Congress Ministers in the Central Government, who were in charge of running the administration, to act according to their judgement. Once they decided in favour of Partition, he did not oppose them, although he never concealed opinion.[71]

His virtual resignation from the decision-making process was also conveyed to Mountbatten in his letter of 11 April 1947.

Gandhi was not in Delhi on Independence Day. On the eve of that day, his mood was bleak. He marked the day with a twenty-four-hour fast, refused to record a message for the *Hindustan Times*, and said 'he had run dry'. He also declined an interview to the BBC and told an emissary 'I forgot English.[72]'

A life spent in promoting fraternity was confronted once again by conflagration of violence that preceded and followed the vivisection of India. It was to be the last challenge of his life.

LIVED AND LED BY EXAMPLE

To us citizens of India, Gandhi is, above all, Father of the Nation. We should therefore turn to him for guidance. What would

[71]Nayar, Pyarelal, 'Going to Wipe their Tears', Jitendra T. Desai, Navajivan Mudranalaya, Ahmedabad, December 2002, https://tinyurl.com/264hwzr3. Accessed on 25 September 2025.

[72]Guha, Ramachandra, *India After Gandhi: The History of the World's Largest Democracy*, Picador, India, 2017, p. 8.

that be? There is a tablet at the Rajghat listing Seven Social Sins. These are simple yet candid and well worth recalling:

1. Wealth without work.
2. Pleasure without conscience.
3. Knowledge without character.
4. Commerce without morality.
5. Science without humanity.
6. Religion without sacrifice.
7. Politics without principle.

Would this be a pertinent ingredient in our resolve of the day? It would please the spirit of Bapu.

This was originally a paper published in IIC's Occasional Publication titled 'The Great Pertinence of Gandhi to India in the 75th Year of Its Independence.'

Chapter 12

Qand-e-Parsi

The late Hashim Abdul Halim was a remarkable personality in terms of his commitments and achievements. Many tributes have been paid to him; I can only add my own and recall what the former Governor of West Bengal Mr Gopalkrishna Gandhi said, that we 'mourn his absence but draw everlasting inspiration from his example of a Marxist mind combining [sic] with a nationalist heart to make the perfect Republican.'

His record of being the Speaker of the West Bengal Legislative Assembly for 29 years in six consecutive terms beginning from 1982 is unquestionably a national record that is unlikely to be equalled and is the best tribute to his sense of correctness. That responsibility is unrelenting and I say this with some personal knowledge as a former Chairman of the Rajya Sabha for a decade.

The late Professor Suniti Kumar Chatterjee's description of an Iranian as 'a learned man who is bold but friendly and whose aim is not to conquer but to convince the opposition' has been applied with justice to him by a contributor to this society's journal published in 2015 who described Abdul Halim sahib as 'a Bengali gentleman with Iranian ethics'.

The Iran Society, Kolkata, depicted in a publication of repute some years back, 'stands like a small hidden oasis of harmony and knowledge seeking. It has remained that way for the last 75 years, untouched by the politics of the day and never straying from the purpose for which it was create.'

This association of ideas and inherited traditions allows me today to speak about India and Iran, or Iran and India, in the wider context of cultural history in the fullest sense of the term. Its basis is neighbourhood whose boundaries have varied with age and time. One Indian ideological dignitary in fashion these days described Iran as 'nothing but the base of Aryabhumi'. The Iranian claims depicted in the sculptures in Persepolis suggest scenes of annual homage and loyalty from provinces of the empire; these included parts of India.

The game of chess in the shape of *chaturanga* was a gift carried by an ambassador to the Iranian court; over time, the Iranian mind modified it into *takhte* that is said to offer a greater negotiating space to the player.

STRINGS OF ATTACHMENT

Our greatest gain perhaps was the Persian language that for centuries remained the court language in different parts of our land and left its impact on regional languages including Bengali. Many centuries back, the poet Hafiz Shirazi was invited to his court by Sultan Ghiyathuddin Sikandar of Bengal. The journey did not materialize and the Sultan received instead an ode that included this often-recited couplet:

Shakkar shikan shawand hami tutiyan-e-Hind
Zeen qand-e-parsi ba Bangala mi-rawad

(All the parrots of India will crack sugar
Through this Persian candy which is going to Bengal)

I might add that poetry, even good poetry, has to ration *qand* since excess of sugar leads to diabetes!

Tradition has it that travel to India was considered a special virtue in educated circles of Iranian society. This is testified to by a couplet of the 15th-century poet Ali Quli Salim:

Neest dar Iran zameen samaan-e-kamal
Ta niyamat su-e-Hindustan hena rangeen na shud

(There exist not in Persia the means of acquiring perfection
Hena does not develop its colour until it comes to India)

These traditions persisted along with geopolitics and statecraft. Wars were fought and peace was made. Nor was the relationship lacking in admonitions and advice, as was rendered by Emperor Jalaluddin Akbar to Shah Abbas the Great. Its universality is evident and has a contemporary relevance: 'In internal affairs, unity is prior to discrepancy and peace is better than war specially as we have always differences of religion until now and considered all classes of people as slaves of God [...] We must be kind to all people who are treasures of god and have mercy on every one, no matter what their religion and idea is.'

The Iranian interest and curiosity about India persist to this day. Many years back, a high-ranking religious personality sought a visa to visit India. His stated purpose was to see a *sanam* (an idol) about which so much is said in Persian literature and poetry!

I recall here a passage in the travelogue of Rabindranath Tagore and his visit in April 1932 to the tomb of the poet Hafiz in Shiraz where the keeper of the mausoleum persuaded him to take the traditional divination or *fal-e-Hafiz* on the volume of the poet's *diwan*. Tagore had, earlier in the day, discussed with the Governor of Shiraz the problem of conflict of faith in multi-religious societies and this was apparently uppermost in his mind when he closed his eyes. The relevant verses on the opened page had an allegorical import that seemed to answer his concern. Its opening line was:

Bood yad ki dar maikad haba-kushayand

(If only the door of the wine houses were to be opened
The knots of problems in our work will be resolved)

Tagore writes that 'friends present there were amazed in noticing the compatibility between my wish and the implied answer. Sitting near the tomb a signal flashed through my mind [...] We were as it were companions in the same tavern...'

I have said enough to show that the Iran Society has a relevant role in furthering and sustaining a relationship that goes beyond the normal state-level cultural exchanges. That it exists in Kolkata is not accidental; this city's relationship with language and culture is well known and is a tribute to Bengali intellectual attainments and their diversity.

THE INDIA-IRAN INTERLINK

Cultural entities and political ones coincide with or overflow their perimeters. This is well reflected at different times in the India-Iran relationship. To a student of geopolitics in the medieval period, the power equation of the Moghuls and the Qutbshahis on the one hand, and of the Moghuls and the Safavids on the other, sheds interesting light on the rules of the game of political chess that have an abiding quality and transcend limitations of time and geography.

Equally evident is the persisting nature of instrumentalities—threat or use of force, interference on pretexts of faith, use and misuse of trade and traders, and attempts to seek 'fifth columns' based on affinities of race or origin—that were used to further policy objectives.

Examples of these propensities can be traced in history and in recent times. The Mogul designs on the Deccan entities, and the latter's close affinity to Persia, inevitably resulted in a clash of interests and perceptions. The Moguls objected to the recitation in Golkonda of the Shah of Persia's name in the Friday prayer sermons. In the War of Succession after Shah Jahan's death, there was clear evidence of Safavid intervention on the side of

Dara Shikoh and, in a counter move, Aurangzeb contemplated but did not pursue an invasion of Persia in alliance with the Uzbegs.

In recent times, tensions developed at the time of the Bangladesh War of 1971 and after the war, Delhi sent P.N. Haksar as special emissary to the Shah of Iran who put a blunt question to the visitor: 'Tell me, quite frankly, is India even remotely interested in the breakup of Pakistan?' Following a long conversation, relations were restored and touched new heights. Another dip followed by restoration was registered in the early 1990s. This continues to recur from time to time followed by correctives emanating from imperatives of geopolitical and economic interests that are appreciated by both sides.

On an earlier occasion and on this platform, in September 2014, I had said much on the imperatives of the present-day relationship. A recent study by an eminent scholar on India and Asian Geopolitics opines, 'for India, Iran is a critical partner in West Asia'; it goes on to say that 'we therefore have good reasons, apart from civilizational and historical inks, to stay clear of attempts to isolate and contain Iran.'

Their relevance is evident and so is the beneficial role of the Iran Society in irrigating the cultural and intellectual landscape for its furthering. This memorial meeting is an important ingredient of it.

This was originally an address at the Hashim Abdul Halim Memorial Lecture organized virtually by Iran Society on 2 November 2021.

Chapter 13

Urdu Journalism

Isi main hogi khuda se bhi guftagoo, Maikash
Ki roz-e-hashr bhi hogi miri zubaan Urdu

It is customary to celebrate anniversaries. Historians say the ancient Egyptians used to celebrate the birth of their Pharaohs, who were considered gods. The practice was inherited by ordinary mortals a few centuries later. It is now widely observed by individuals, families and countries. This year we Indians are celebrating the 75th anniversary of our Independence.

So, the decision to mark and celebrate the bicentenary of Urdu journalism is logical and necessary considering the role it has played in the formation of public perceptions in the last two hundred years of our history, a period that has witnessed great social and political turmoil in our society.

It is insufficiently known that Persian was for centuries the official language in many parts of India and the first Persian newspaper in the world was published by Raja Rammohan Roy in 1822. Urdu followed it closely and Harihar Datta published *Ja-i-Jahan-Numa* in the same year.

Except for the last 75 years, the bulk of these two centuries were under the period of foreign rule with all the restrictions that went with it. A methodology to overcome it was also crafted and was expressed in the couplet:

Khincho na kamanon ko na talwar nikalo
Jab top muqabil ho to akhbar nikalo

Publications nevertheless were subject to stringent rules. The story is told of Ram Prasad Bismil's couplet that was considered seditious:

Sar faroshi ki tamanna phir hamare dil main hai
Dekhna hai zour kitna bazo-u-e-qatil main hai

A timely intervention by a literate and sympathetic magistrate saved the day by his suggestion that the term used in the first line was not *hamare* but *aashiqon ke*!

The seriousness with which scrutiny of poetic matter was pursued is evident from the work undertaken by Dr Rajesh Kumar Perti, former Director General of the National Archives, in his diligently compiled collection of poems—*Ashob*—that were considered seditious and confiscated and preserved in the India Office in London. One of these poems, 'Khak-e-Hind', has these couplets:

Barson se ho raha hai barham samaan hamara
Dunya se mit raha hai naam-o-nishan hamara
Kuch kum nahi ajal se khwab-e-geraan hamara
Ab laash be-kafan hai Hindostan hamara
Bulbul ko gul mubarak, gul ko chaman mubarak
Hum baaghiyon ko apna pyara watan mubarak

Times changed and we are now a free country. The role and responsibilities of journalism in a democracy is to inform, educate, guide and entertain. Each of these is a valid and essential function, more so in modern societies whose size and numbers need means of communication other than direct face-to-face ones. This is sustained by the law.

The Supreme Court has held that 'the fundamental freedom under Article 19(1)(a) can be reasonably restricted only for the purposes mentioned in Articles 19(2) and the restriction must be justified on the anvil of necessity and not of convenience or expediency. Open criticism of government policies and operations is not a ground for restricting expression. We must practise tolerance for the views of others. Intolerance is as dangerous to democracy as to the person himself.

This in theory is impeccable, less so in practice, and we come across instances of it particularly in the Urdu press in Jammu and Kashmir.

THE BATTLES OF URDU JOURNALISM

The Urdu press is the third largest in the country after Hindi and English. Urdu newspapers and periodicals are published in 16 states of the Union and one union territory.

According to the Census of India 2011 and in terms of speakers' strength in Scheduled Languages, Urdu ranks 7th at 50.7 million, after Hindi, Bengali, Marathi, Telegu, Tamil and Gujarati. It had a speaker's strength of 4.19 million; this figure was 52.5 million in 1981, 51.8 million in 1991 and 5.01 million in 2011.

This decline, in a framework of overall increase of population and more specific demographic data, raises a question. Why is the number of Urdu speakers declining when the areas and groups generally associated with the language have registered normal increases in population?

Why has this happened? Does it suggest a pattern of language abandonment? An explanation in a wider context was given by Professor Abram de Swan in a paper published in the *European Review* in October 2004:

> People who abandon their native tongue do so because they move elsewhere or take up something else and in this new existence they have higher expectations of a different

> language. Or they neglect it because another language is preferred at school, by public authorities, or in courts of law, and their own language is treated with disdain. Or they have to stop using it because they are ruled by another nation that imposes its language on them, and, having lost heart, they no longer take care to preserve their own language.[73]

He went on to add that since 'every language is a product of the collective creativity of people expressed over hundreds or thousands of years, its disappearance is an irreversible loss of culture.'[74]

Where then do we look for an explanation for the decline of Urdu speakers? Since language is principally a matter of affiliation and usage, giving it up is unlikely to be voluntary or an act of 'enlightenment' and must necessarily emanate from some form of compulsion or necessity.

Hence the key to our primary question has to be sought amidst the factors cited by Professor de Swan, and of the three possible situations visualized by him, the answer seems to be in the second—namely, language at school level and in use by public authorities.

Two sets of facts shed light on it:

- In a question answered in the Rajya Sabha on 12 August 2011, the Ministry of Human Resource Development stated that Urdu was not being taught in Kendriya Vidyalayas in various states since in none of them twenty or more students opted for the language, adding that for the same reason no posts of Urdu teachers were sanctioned.
- The simple conclusion to be drawn is that Urdu-knowing

[73]De Swaan, Abram, *European Review*, 2004.

[74]Ibid.

> students do not make it to Kendriya Vidyalayas in the minimum numbers prescribed. The data has other implications since these schools are primarily for transferable central government employees

Some years back, the late scholar Dr Omar Khalidi had examined the state of Urdu literacy in India as gauged through school education and raised five questions:

- How many students in primary schools are having Urdu as the language of instruction?
- How many are learning Urdu as one of the subjects under the three-language (or four-language) formula?
- Have the various levels of government—central, state and local—facilitated or obstructed learning of Urdu in various states?
- To what can we attribute the uneven levels of Urdu literacy in various states?
- What are the other institutions, besides schools run by the state, involved in promoting Urdu literacy?

Khalidi's conclusions on the first two questions, based on available official data, revealed that Urdu literacy in terms of Urdu-medium enrolment in primary-secondary schools is highest in Maharashtra and Bihar, less so in Karnataka and Andhra, and least in Uttar Pradesh and Delhi. In terms of percentages of total enrolment for the year 2007–08, it was 6.53 in Maharashtra, 5.2 in Bihar, 5.9 in Karnataka, 2.8 in Andhra, 1.0 in Delhi and 0.40 in Uttar Pradesh.

The answer to the third and fourth questions requires delving into recent history. Here I can do no better than to recall Jawaharlal Nehru's own assessment. In a confidential letter to chief ministers on 16 July 1953, he spoke of 'a pettiness in mind, a narrowness in outlook and an immaturity' that characterized 'a deliberate attempt to push out Urdu which is spoken and written by a large number of people.'[75] This was repeated two weeks later in a letter on August 1:

> We encourage the smallest tribal language in its own area, but many of us resent even the mention of Urdu, and yet Urdu is very much a child of India and is a vital and graceful aspect of our many-sided culture. I am deeply grieved at this narrowness of outlook which so frequently comes in our way...[76]

Nehru reiterated his views in the Hyderabad session of the All India Congress Committee in October the same year.

A Union Home Ministry circular of July 1958 mentioned the need to provide Urdu language teaching at the primary stage to children having it as their mother tongue. It did not refer to Article 350A of the Constitution nor did it invoke Article 347.

The American scholar Paul Brass, in his 1974 book *Language, Religion and Politics in North India,* shed much light on the policy and procedural methodology by which some states succeeded 'in diverting large number of Urdu speakers'[77] from the path of education in their mother tongue.

Narrow political perceptions and mistaken identification of language with a community thus led to a unilingual approach and prevailed over the linguistic diversity of a plural society and the ethos of the Constitution.

In 1972, the Government of India Resolution that set up the Gujral Committee to ascertain ways for the promotion and development of Urdu stated that 'Urdu is not the concern of any one State Government or of any community. The responsibility for its development has also to be shared by the

---

[75]Nehru, Jawaharlal, *Letters to Chief Ministers 1947-1964, 1958-64, Vol. 5,* Gopalaswami Parthasarathi (ed.), Oxford University Press, 1989.

[76]Ibid.

[77]Brass, Paul, *Language, Religion and Politics in North India*, iUniverse, 1974.

Central Government.'[78] Its recommendations (1975), as also of the Ali Sardar Jaafri Committee in 1990, show the extent to which they were implemented meaningfully. Nor has the National Council for Promotion of Urdu Language, established in 1990, registered a significant success in its primary objective.

THE SUSTENANCE PRINCIPLE

Lamentation about the past is relevant only to draw lessons from it. Our concern today should be with the present, and the future. Where does Urdu stand now on the basis of the data cited above? What is its place in our social and cultural life, our political and economic life? How can its attributed affiliation to a specific community, with all its unstated suggestions, be overcome to recapture its rightful place in the kaleidoscope of languages and cultural patterns of India? How can it be rejuvenated, its future be made livelier?

On one plane, official acknowledgement of Urdu is extended with unfailing regularity. Anniversaries are observed, patronage given to 'mushairas'. Its limitations are also obvious:

'Zubaan ki yaad to qayam rahi hai, taraqqi nahin hoti'.

Ghalib jise kehte hain Urdu ka hi shair tha
Urdu pe sitam karke Ghalib pe karam kyon ho

A commentator has observed that 'Urdu has been kept alive by the Hindi cinema, FM radio, madrassas and occasional recitation of couplets in Parliament'. He drew attention to Professor Gopi Chand Narang's remark that 'Urdu is like a patient on oxygen at the fag end of his life. This is the last generation of Urdu.'[79]

---

[78]Rajya Sabha Debates, https://tinyurl.com/kyzhsbjj. Accessed on 18 September 2025.

[79]Nazli, Taiyaba, 'Predicament of the Learners of Urdu Medium Schools "A

Bollywood films played a major role in keeping alive the usage of Urdu. The historian Ramachandra Guha has observed that 'at the time of independence and perhaps for a century before that the pre-eminent language of poetry was Urdu.' Others like Ira Bhaskar and Richard Allen have shed light on the points of intersection between history, culture, language, community and contemporary tensions, to demonstrate its 'cultural and political value [...] in the plural and multicultural imagination of India.'

The role of *madaaris* is noteworthy. They have sustained Urdu in difficult times in the context of their curricula of studies and have helped take it to a segment of the younger generation. By the same token, however, the effort has been community-specific and confined to those of its members who preferred a madrasa, generally for economic reasons, to normal, state-run schools. At the same time, confining Urdu to the madaaris also has an impact on what is historically an essentially secular, occasionally libertarian temper of the language.

Languages are learnt and sustained for a variety of reasons. They are imbibed firstly at home as mother tongue and supplemented through primary (and secondary) schooling in it. This necessitates availability of schools, textbooks and teachers provided either by the state or local authority or through community efforts. Secondly, languages are learnt through economic compulsions and in quest of economic opportunities. It implies participation in wider and prevalent community patterns of education and employability and the requisite effort by society to make available educational institutions and teachers. In the third place, a language may be learnt as a preferred elective for social or religious prestige or academic excellence.

The challenge for a declining language is thus at two levels.

Critical Observation"', *Scholarly Research Journal for Interdisciplinary Studies*, Vol.9/68, 2021, pp. 16364–16374.

The child's inherited awareness of the mother tongue is part of his/her personal, social and cultural identity and has to be shaped and consolidated by structured instruction to enable him or her to proceed from illiteracy to basic literacy. Thereafter, the instrumental motivation and contours of language revival must necessarily be shaped by economic factors. In most multilingual societies (including India), the latter is a function of dominant language for administration, business and inter-regional and international communications. The picture here is evident, and fully accepted.

The situation is different with regard to the mother tongue. It is a fundamental right of citizens, under Article 29, to conserve their distinct language and script. The objective of Article 350A—'for every State and every local authority within the State to provide adequate facilities for instruction in the mother tongue at the primary stage of education to children belonging to linguistic minority groups'—however remains unachieved for a great number of Urdu-speaking children. In some cases, their linguistic identity is overlooked or ignored; in others, primary-school arrangements remain non-functional by the absence of Urdu language teachers and textbooks. The persistence of these defaults raises doubts about the sincerity of the effort.

The conclusion is inescapable that this is a case of multiple failures: on the part of the state in its constitutional obligations, of the Urdu-speaking communities in their cultural duty to be assertive in seeking to learn and sustain the language, and of individual families for not making the additional effort required for doing so.

THE FIGHT TO STAY ALIVE

What then is to be done? The Senegalese poet Baba Dioum has observed thus: 'In the end we will conserve only what we love.

We love only what we understand and we will understand only what we are taught.'

The imperative need is to find ways of teaching Urdu to those who call it their mother tongue. This task has to begin in primary school and should continue, at least in part, in the secondary school. The problem would be resolved if in the Three Language Formula, evolved and accepted under the National Language Policy, Urdu is assigned the same status as its sister Indian languages. This, regrettably, is not forthcoming in government schools in some states, and in others due to tardiness in recruitment of teachers and publication of textbooks, etc. The deficiencies in the implementation of safeguards for linguistic minorities in different states are recorded with some precision in reports of the Commissioner for Linguistic Minorities, asserting that 'the constitutional safeguards provided for the linguistic minorities can only become real when there is necessary supportive legislation.'

Until more assertive state action is taken, the only alternative is to organize efforts at the family and Urdu-speaking community level. The experience of declining-language communities elsewhere in the world would be relevant in this context. A good example is the practice of the Jewish community undertaking weekend instruction in Hebrew in the United States. Other examples of successful language revival are Catalan in Spain and French in Canada.

Alongside, the need to keep alive the efforts to make the state honour constitutional obligations in regard to those who claim Urdu as their mother tongue has to be galvanized. Public opinion and electoral pressures do produce results, as has happened in several states of the Indian Union. We have at all times to remember that justice is the first of the four principles enshrined in the Preamble of our Constitution and, as the philosopher John Rawls put it, 'the rights secured by justice are not subject to political bargaining or to the calculus of social interests.'

There is, nevertheless, some silver lining on the horizon. Urdu newspapers and magazines have survived the decline and shown signs of a revival. Corporate media has shown interest in the Urdu press. Books in Urdu continue to be published and are inexpensively priced. Several Urdu television channels (apart from Doordarshan-Urdu) have come into existence and seem to survive commercially. The music industry continues to prosper on Urdu ghazals, songs and qawwalis.

There are also signs of a desire among the youth to learn the language. Apart from the standard postgraduate course in language and literature, the Urdu department of the University of Delhi now has a Certificate and a Diploma course with high enrolment.

One other factor of relevance needs a mention. Urdu is now an international language and is being studied and promoted beyond the Indian subcontinent. The internet is assisting the effort in good measure. It would indeed be a tragedy of profound dimensions if the language should regress and disappear in the land of its birth.

The question in the final analysis also pertains to our perception of Indian pluralism and of the ambit of Indian culture. Is it to be inclusive or exclusive? Has it to be characterized by catholicity of approach or otherwise? Do we retain what has enriched it in the past and continues to do so today, or discard for considerations emanating from an illiberal outlook?

Kisi bhi shama se be-zaar ho kyon koi parvana
Yeh kya is daur ka diwana-pun hai hum nahin samjhe

This was originally an address at the bicentenary celebrations of Urdu journalism on 30 March 2022, at India Islamic Centre, New Delhi. The Urdu text 'As Delivered on Urdu Journalism on March 30, 2022' was published in the Urdu daily Inquilab *on 30–31 March 2022.*

Chapter 14

An Unending Mission

Jahan jaeen wahan tera fasana chair dete hain
Koi mehfil ho tera rang-e-mehfil yaad aata hai

Of all the human sentiments, nostalgia about youth is perhaps the most natural because it is a mix of pleasant happenings of the past. Memory is selective and recall voluntary; achievements become larger than life and moments of truth glossed over. Old albums are searched for a cherished group photograph and its discovery brings forth joyful recollections.

I can recall my time at AMU in a manner that is unique. I have done likewise for the period I spent in the university as a student and many decades later as vice chancellor. In the latter responsibility, I discovered that much had changed. I shared my agony with a very senior, long retired Aligarian. He answered me in a couplet by Allama Iqbal:

Waa-e-nakami mata-e-karwaan jata raha
Kaarwan ke dil se ehsas-e-ziyan jata raha.

He was both right and not right. Times had changed and so had some of the purposes of existence. What had not changed was an ingrained human desire for seeking success.

The audience before me today, of different generations, represents a good example of success. What motivated you? At what stage of your AMU period did the process begin or take shape? Did the urge dawn post-AMU? Where and when did this journey begin?

The Federation of Aligarh Alumni Associations states as its objectives an 'over-arching mission to promote modern education and support students in advancing their professional goals.'

Some home truths have to be faced. Muslims in India, over 15.3 per cent of our population and numbering around 200 million, are not homogenous in terms of class and caste. Data on the marginalization of Muslims in urban India, where a substantial majority of them reside, sheds much light on this. A few years back, an eminent sociologist studied the specifics of Muslim presence in ten of the biggest urban Muslim conglomerations; this included Aligarh and two of its localities: Shah Jamal and Sir Syed Nagar. We are familiar with the contrasting social characteristics of both.

In October 2008, I was invited to address the World Summit of AMU Alumni. I opined on that occasion that Sir Syed Ahmad Khan's mission in 1875 succeeded in highlighting the centrality of modern education that to him meant the spirit of rational thinking and scientific inquiry. He succeeded to a point but in the context of his times failed to go beyond it. I discerned four reasons for it:

- a failure to appreciate the need for universal education, particularly at the primary stage
- a failure to appreciate the need for women's education and its relevance for educating new generations
- a failure to adopt creative ventures in education independent of government agencies, as was done by other communities in India
- a failure to appreciate the need for organized philanthropy

I suggest that it should become the catalyst for a corrective, beginning at the grassroots level. I am aware that this will come across a mental block since the famed Muslim egalitarianism on display in the mosque tends to be forgotten beyond its confines.

A good contemporary example proving the contrary is before us in the Sikh community and its educational and philanthropic institutions all over India. Equally relevant in New York and elsewhere in the United States is the Jewish community.

Why have we failed to do likewise, apart from giving out eloquent expressions of grievances? Lack of resources is not the answer; perhaps it lies in the absence of a sense of commitment.

The Aligarh fraternity should therefore seek to locate in their own way micro projects for primary education, facilitate to the possible extent their viability, and propagate the need to inculcate a spirit of competitiveness, so that it can draw maximum benefits from government scholarship schemes, seek equity (not concessions) from the government and mobilize opinion from religious endowments (Awqaf) for educational and professional institutions whose focus at all times should be on quality and relevance.

I am aware that things are changing, that much good work is being done now, particularly in southern Indian states and in Maharashtra. Commendable initiatives have been taken to establish medical and engineering colleges. Yet, this does not fill the gap of over half a century; nor does it focus on the inadequacy of the feedstock of competent school-leaving graduates who can avail of these facilities without seeking reservations that are becoming increasingly difficult legally.

Official and NGO data shows Muslims to be almost at the bottom of the social and educational pyramid. A resultant handicap is the low though improving number of Muslims succeeding in competitive examinations for middle- and senior-level government jobs. This is all the more necessary because a subtle display of prejudice or discrimination is evident in some key areas of governance and has to be overcome by proven competence.

Allow me to take the liberty of suggesting that in small groups and in their own chosen areas, we must take the initiative of opening and supporting primary and secondary schools for the children of the least privileged segments of Muslim community, daily wage earners, who otherwise are too busy with the problems of existence to worry about educating their children and who would be happy enough if a child at the age of 10 or 12 becomes a wage earner, thereby lessening the burden on parents.

THE PURPOSE OF THIS LIFE

Allow me to touch upon another aspect of AMU's mission. Its purpose was, and should remain, modern education and rational thinking. How do we interpret it in the second decade of the 21st century and in a fast-changing world?

What characterizes it individually and collectively, more so for those who travelled beyond the shores of India and are now gainfully employed and settled here? A visitor from the land of their origin is expected to say some things about it.

India is a status quo power and does not seek territories of others. It is committed to working for a peaceful world and a peaceful South Asia. Doubts about these commitments are raised at times and are responded to appropriately. We participate regularly in all the activities of the global community including UN Peacekeeping. We hold that new technologies for the benefit of humankind are shared globally and must not be monopolized.

Today the global scene stands transformed. Two decades of the 21st century have witnessed changes in power structures. As with earlier bipolarity, unipolarity too has collapsed. The United States, despite the size of its economy and technological superiority, is a chastened power. Europe has discovered its strength in a non-homogenous European Union. The Soviet Union has been replaced by Russia and a number of its erstwhile units are seeking their own place in the sun, unsure of their affinity to the former arrangement. The Arab world, linguistic affinity apart, hardly agrees on any core unifying agenda. Israel has succeeded in securing its place in the sub-region.

For us, the priority has to be the immediate neighbourhood in South Asia where the progress of regional cooperation has been tardy. Relations with Bangladesh, Bhutan, Nepal, Sri Lanka, Afghanistan and Maldives are in good shape but problems persist in two areas.

China is a neighbour with whom we have a long border with disputed segments as well as environmental issues of a complex nature. It is militarily and economically stronger. There have been periods of military confrontation followed by commitments to maintain the status quo. There exists a vibrant trading relationship, adverse yet beneficial to segments of our economy. China's economic progress is impressive but it is slowing down. Its political structure and social cohesion are impressive. Its plans to expand influence on land and sea are at times unnerving. On the other hand, the outside world is barely aware of its diversities and its domestic tensions and problems.

Pakistan is a neighbour with some affinities. Here the subjective is as relevant as the objective. The legacy of 1947 and perceptions emanating from it remain relevant in varying degrees with actors and spectators. It is a nuclear power and uses this status to its benefit. At the same time, wisdom and prudence make a normal relationship unavoidable despite political and other predilections.

Our relations with the United States in all fields have made good progress in recent decades. It is also reflected in the presence of the second largest expatriate community here. Its members are happy and gainfully employed, to the benefit of both societies.

The United States is a vibrant democracy. The American social scene is open and diverse. This diversity at times allows for giving vent to unsocial and intolerant sentiments. Two Indian newspapers, *The Economic Times* and *The Indian Express*, carried reports a few days back of a survey of hate crimes against Asian Americans and of 'Indian Americans regularly encountering discrimination'. *The Indian Express* also cited a *New York Times* report. The survey was undertaken by credible scholars and can be read in full on the website of Carnegie Endowment for International Peace under the caption 'Social Realities of American Indians'.[80]

These attitudes regretfully can also be found in other countries against minority segments of population on grounds of colour, race, religion, food habits, and even a mixture of these under the general category of being the 'other'. Above all, they exist in our own land in discriminatory attitudes and even hatred against religious or regional minorities. So, the experience is not unique; it is nevertheless unwelcome and despicable whenever and wherever it surfaces.

How do we react to them? Do we reply in kind? Is it likely to be productive in the face of various odds that may surface?

The alternative is to resort to law and to legal remedies, to reasonable contestation, and to support of saner opinion in societies. These exist in American and Indian societies and have been in evidence here in recent months. The process may be time-consuming but is unavoidable.

Let me recall a lesson learnt in AMU:

- An Aligarian does not forget the lessons of civility.
- A good citizen too resorts to it in times good and difficult.
- A good Muslim will at all times recall what is said in the Book:

---

[80]Badrinatham, Sumitra, Devesh Kapur, Jonathan Kay and Milan Vaishnav, 'Social Realities of Indian Americans: Results from the 2020 Indian American Attitudes Survey', *Carnegie Endowment for International Peace*, 9 June 2021, https://tinyurl.com/wd87w86u. Accessed on 29 October 2025.

> O ye who believe! Seek help with patient Perseverance and Prayer: for God with those who patiently persevere
> (Quran 2.153)

This patience and perseverance are also required of a good citizen.

This was originally an address at the Federation of Amu Alumni, New York, organized virtually on 26 June 2021.

Chapter 15

Communal Discord and Its Social Cost

January 30 is an important date in the calendar of our society. It is the day of the martyrdom of Mahatma Gandhi, the day a fanatic propelled by an extremist ideology resorted to violence to silence him.

The world lamented and people expressed grief in their own ways. The poet Josh Malihabadi did it in a long poem that had both remorse and satire:

Dehr par teri shahadat ne ye sabit kar diya
Had se barh kar nek hone kis qadar hai na-rawa
Qatilon main qatl-e-insani pe rona jurm hai
Tukhm-me neki sarzamin-e-dil main bona jurm hai

Gandhi died as he lived: dedicated to his principles, to his own version of modernity premised on Ahimsa. On his last birthday on 2 October 1947, his request to visitors was to pray 'either the present conflagration should end or He should take me away. I do not wish another birthday to overtake me in an India still in flames.'[81]

Mahatma Gandhi sought concord in a world of discord. He had witnessed the latter in all its dimensions and consciously worked to counter it.

---

[81]Ashraf, Ajaz, 'Gandhi Jayanti: As nation prepares to mark 150 years of the Mahatma, let's not forget his darkest hour', *Firstpost*, 2 October 2018, https://tinyurl.com/mr2u7epc. Accessed on 5 September 2025.

It has to be admitted that he failed and that the virus of discord and hatred has continued to determine public perceptions.

What is India? The poet Raghupati Rai Firaq shed light on the process of the formation of India:

Sar zamin-e-Hind par aqwal-e-aalam ke Firaq
Qafle baste gaye, Hindostaan banta gaya[82]

What was the character of the end product? A poet shed light on it in a couplet:

Kehte hain bhai bhai hain ahle-watan tamaam
Phirte hain aasteenon main khanzar liye hue

It was thought that the values prescribed in the Constitution, particularly the principle of fraternity in the Preamble, and of the duty in Article 51A(e) 'to promote harmony and the spirit of common brotherhood among all the people of India transcending religious, linguistic and regional and regional or sectional diversities,' would induce the required correctives.

The Indian reality however was found to be more complex. It was summed up by a poet of our times, Amir Chand Bahar:

Insaan hi insaan se badzan kyon hai
Insaan hi insaan ka dushman kyon hai
Kehne ko to Ram Ram kehte hain sabhi
Kardar se har admi Raawan kyon hai?

CHANNELS AND CHALLENGES

Communal disharmony had afflicted India before, and since, Independence. Its seriousness took time to be recognized. Finally, and after the experience of several decades, the government

---

[82]Gorakhpuri, Firaq, 'सर-ज़मीन-ए-हिंदपरअक़्वाम-ए-आलमके "फ़िराक़"', *Rekhta*, https://tinyurl.com/4fbk2t9r. Accessed on 5 September 2025.

constituted the National Integration Council in 1960 and the National Foundation for Communal Harmony in 1992. Various other legislative and administrative measures were taken from time to time. A Communal Violence (Prevention, Control and Rehabilitation of Victims) Bill was introduced before 2014 but has remained unattended. The hesitation in accepting this as a problem is itself indicative of the mindset.

Incidents of violence can and do happen sporadically. Organized violence, however, is another matter and results from hate that is nurtured purposefully. Instances of the latter have occurred in our society and invariably involve political planning and administrative connivance. They are sustained by administrative and civil society facilities. An answer to this mindset was given in a popular couplet:

Mazhab nahin sikath aaapus main bair rakhna
Hindi hain hum watan hai Hindostaan hamara[83]

The attitude of evading, or facilitating, the issue however has deeper causes. An eminent sociologist has shed light on it: 'The empirical reality of India does not suit the institution of the nation-state which relentlessly pursues cultural homogenisation in the name of cultural consolidation,' and that 'groups and communities unwilling to surrender their cultural identity to avail of equality in citizenship entitlements should be coerced to do so in the name of national integration.' The way out 'is the creation of a nation-state which recognises cultural identity and celebrates it.'

Thus, the challenge to our liberal polity established by the Constitution is both ideological and practical. The latter can be countered by a corrective administered by the electoral process, as has been attempted from time to time. The former, on the other

[83]Iqbal, Allama, 'मज़हब नहीं सिखाता आपस में बैर रखना', *Rekhta*, https://tinyurl.com/fmzprswu. Accessed on 5 September 2025.

hand, requires a careful examination of the philosophic backdrop, ideological pronouncements and terminological sophistry of the political hypothesis that succeeded at the polls in 2014 and again in 2019, and which is optimistic about the immediate and foreseeable future.

To this end, it puts across a (slanted) view that while diversity is inherent in the Indian scheme of creation and is the manifestation of a cosmic entity in different forms, its acceptance in the context of the Bharatiya view of life requires the exclusion of all alien views.

In the process it seeks to erase other influences down the ages, including the existential reality of over a thousand years of Indian history, and to impose an imagined version of cultural homogeneity with all its political connotations, leading to what has been called by informed observers an 'ethnic democracy'. Do we need to bear this cost?

The challenge is real; it is also urgent. It has to be met in terms of ideas, practices and day-to-day behaviour. This is what the poets advocated; this can be turned into reality by public action.

PART II

ZONES OF TURBULENCE

Chapter 16

A 'Mythistory' of Our Times

Rarely has social media summed up a situation so succinctly: according to the Urban Dictionary, the noun Israel *'got israeled'* as a verb to mean when someone is asked to share something of yours, then claims it as their own, and takes it for themselves[84].

How, and where, did the idea of a Jewish national home arise and take shape, since recorded history on the matter is somewhat hazy?

It became relevant in the second half of the nineteenth century in Central and Eastern Europe in the lands between Vienna and Odessa. It grew uneasily on the fringes of German nationalism and reached the lively cultural marketplaces of the Yiddish population. Zionism was part of this resurgence in Europe and coincided with the rise of other nationality-awakening ideologies on the continent. It was triggered by popular pogroms directed at the Jews who were compelled to migrate to safer lands. Some went to America; others, less than three per cent, ended up in Ottoman-Palestine.

Leo Motzkin, an early Zionist ideologue, summed up the approach: 'our thought is that the colonization of Palestine has to go in two directions—Jewish settlement in Eretz Israel and the resettlement of the Arabs of Eretz Israel in areas outside the country.'

---

[84]Urban Dictionary, https://tinyurl.com/3dwdasu4. Accessed on 18 September 2025.

The future of Palestine was the subject of intense discussion throughout the twentieth century. The closing years of World War I brought forth a new set of imperatives. These were summed up by the historian Arnold Toynbee in the following manner:

> The Balfour Declaration of 2nd November 1917 was the winning card in a sordid contest between the two sets of belligerents in the First World War for winning the support of the Jews in Germany, Austria-Hungary, and—most important of all—in the United States.[85]

The instrument crafted was 'a Mandate under the Covenant of the League of Nations'. The responsibility for implementing the Mandate was given to Great Britain.

At the start of the Mandate in 1918, 'the Arab Palestinians amounted to more than 90 per cent of the population of the country'; in 1947, the Arabs numbered 1,237,000 and the Jews 625,000. This increase in numbers, Toynbee concluded, 'was imposed on the Palestinian Arabs by the British military power.'[86]

Towards the end of World War II, Britain referred the matter to the United Nations, which in Resolution 181 recommended a partition by a majority vote, with an international regime for Jerusalem. It was supported by both the United States and the USSR.

Odd Arne Westad records in his *History of the Cold War* President Truman's argument that an early recognition 'was necessary for both Cold War and domestic policy reasons,'[87] though in his personal diary he made some uncomplimentary remarks about the Jews.

In the final stages of the British mandate, illegal migration

---

[85]Toynbee, A.J., 'Foreword', *The Palestine Diary, 1914-1945*, by Robert John and Sami Hadawi, New World Press, New York, 1970.

[86]Ibid.

[87]Westad, Odd Arne, *The Cold War: A World History*, Penguin, Ireland, 2018.

became the main form of Jewish entry into Palestine, with Jewish groups opting for 'the scientific use of terror to break the will of liberal rulers'[88]. The United States gave a helping hand. Palestinian bewilderment, and the ineptness of the Arab governments, did the rest.

The State of Israel came into existence on 14 May 1948 and '750,000 Palestinians fled from the Israeli-held territory'[89].

The war that followed resulted in UNGA Resolution 194 (1949), the emergence of Israel as a state and eventually of Resolution 3236 (1974) reaffirming the inalienable rights of the Palestinian people to self-determination, national independence and sovereignty, and the right of the Palestinians to return to their homes and property.

Since the Palestinians were a majority in the mandated territory, the task before the Zionist leadership was to turn them into a minority. Writing in 1968, Toynbee observed that 'the reason why Israel exists today and why 1,500,000 Palestinian Arabs are refugees is that, for thirty years, Jewish immigration was imposed on the Palestinian Arabs by British military power until the immigrants were sufficiently numerous and sufficiently well-armed to fend for themselves with tanks and planes of their own.'[90]

Thus was God`s promise to the Jews given a concrete shape and the Palestinian Arabs were 'made to pay for the genocide of Jews in Europe which was committed by Germans not Arabs.'

The state of Israel came into existence on 14 May 1948 and its first Declaration proclaimed that 'The Land of Israel was the

---

[88]Gibson, Geoffrey, 'History-terrorism-terror: Paris and Terror VI—Terror in History', 16 February 2015, https://tinyurl.com/349zc5xe. Accessed on 5 September 2025.

[89]'Israel and Palestinians: History of the Conflict Explained', *BBC*, 8 August 2025, https://tinyurl.com/2vvjzt6h. Accessed on 5 September 2025.

[90]Ibid.

birthplace of the Jewish people. Here their spiritual, religious and political identity was shaped.'

The results of this exercise have been summed up by an Israeli scholar: 'The greatest achievement of Zionism is the creation of an Israeli identity, which reflects the fact that the dream of a new nation, a new human reality, has been realized. [...] Israeli culture and identity are the progeny of Zionism.'[91]

For many years, this standard Israeli account of the character of the Arab-Israeli conflict remained largely uncontested outside the Arab world.

The reality of occupation, however, was different. In December 2023, Oxford historian Avi Shlaim critically observed that between 1967 and 2005, 'a few thousand Israeli settlers controlled 25 percent of the territory, 40 percent of the arable land, and the largest share of the desperately scarce water resources.'[92]

CHOICE OF A NO SOLUTION

Bilateral and multilateral efforts in subsequent decades to seek a solution to the resulting problems brought forth no compromise. On the contrary, and early in 2018, Israel's ruling Likud Party unanimously endorsed a resolution calling for the annexation of West Bank settlements, and the Public Security Minister Gilad Erdan declared: 'We are telling the world that it doesn't matter what the nations of the world say. The time has come to express our biblical right to the land.'[93]

---

[91]Beit-Hallahmi, Benjamin, 'Naming Norms and Identity Choices in Israel', *Jewish Survival: The Identity Problem at the Close of the Twentieth Century*, Ernest Krausz and Gitta Tulea (eds.), Routledge, 1998.

[92]Shlaim, Avi, 'War on Gaza: Netanyahu, Hamas and the origins of the 2023 Nakba war', *Middle East Eye*, 21 December 2023, https://tinyurl.com/wpm9x4d5. Accessed on 5 September 2025.

[93]Pappe, Ilan, 'Examining Ten Myths about Israel', *American Council for Judaism*,

The fortieth anniversary of the establishment of the Israeli state, however, and the release of official documents coincided with the efforts by Israeli scholars to challenge it. The historian Ilan Pappe contested 'the Ten Myths' about the origin and identity of the contemporary state Israel. Five of these related to the origins: (a) that Palestine was an empty land, (b) that the Jews were a people without land, (c) that Zionism is Judaism, (d) that Zionism is not Colonialism, and (e) that the Palestinians left their land in 1948.

Subsequent writings, and official Israeli assertions, have confirmed the validity of these questions.

The war of June 1967 changed the landscape to Israel's benefit. It was followed by UNSC resolutions 242 (1967) and 338 (1973). In 1974, the PLO was officially recognized by the Arab League and the United Nations General Assembly as the 'sole legitimate representative of the Palestinian people'[94], and was invited to participate in all UN activities under observer status. The Arab states, after much meandering, developed a common position in the Arab League Declaration of March 2002. This was followed a few months later by the Palestinian Non-Paper (12 June 2002) outlining a vision for Permanent Status Negotiations based on it and stating that 'the border between the state of Palestine and the state of Israel will be the June 4 1967 Armistice Line.'

Some light on this was shed by Benjamin Beit-Hallahmi of Haifa University in *Original Sins: Reflections on the History of Zionism and Israel*: Out of the original sins of the world against the Jews grew the original sins of Zionism against the Palestinians. Looking at the future, he argued that the main obstacles to a solution have to do with exorcising the past, admitting past and present injustice for one side; forgiving the past, and the present

---

15 February 2018, https://tinyurl.com/bpafdcn6. Accessed on 5 September 2025.

[94]Palestine Liberation Organisation (PLO), https://tinyurl.com/3mfkkpk3. Accessed on 18 September 2025.

for the other. The Israelis' problem is asking for forgiveness; the Palestinians' the readiness to forgive [...] Israelis seem to be trapped in a peculiar and impossible situation. Any concession to the Palestinians may lead to the unravelling of the whole Zionist enterprise.[95]

An assessment of the balance of forces by former negotiator and diplomat Prof. Itamar Rabinovich of Hebrew University was realistic:

> The military might that Israel displayed in June 1967 convinced the Arabs that they could not reasonably hope to end the conflict through a military victory [...] The effect of the 1967 defeat was qualitatively different from that of the defeats of 1948 and 1956 [...] In the Arabs' ensuing soul-searching, several alternatives were fiercely debated [...] but a recommendation to seek a political settlement based on a historic compromise was not made.[96]

Further turmoil, regional and global, including the arrival in Israel of nearly a million immigrants from the former Soviet Union, and the long and profound effect of the *intifada* on the Israeli public, eventually led to the Madrid Conference of October 1991. The letter of invitation to invitees did not include the phrase 'territories for peace' but was mentioned in the letters of assurance addressed to the Arab invitees.

THE MANY PLAYERS AND THEIR CARDS

The event of 7 October initiated by Hamas, and mistakenly depicted as 'terrorist', was a logical outcome of the Israeli political

---

[95]Beit-Hallahmi, Benjamin, *Original Sins: Reflections on the History of Zionism and Israel,* Olive Branch Press, 1996.

[96]Rabinovich, Itamar, *Waging Peace: Israel and the Arabs, 1948-2003,* Princeton University Press, 2004.

establishment's disavowal of an effective two-state outcome (or a one-state solution based on equality of all residents). This, together with the proclaimed Israeli aspiration of a full annexation of Gaza and the West Bank, and the resultant increasing popularity of Hamas in both the West Bank and Gaza—and of the reluctance of the US to persuade the Israeli establishment towards it—made this a logical outcome.

The Israeli argument, and the substance of Netanyahu's reasoning, is guarantee of a continued Israeli control over the majority of West Bank, its land, water, internal and external movement and transportation, and overriding security. This in effect is a recipe for preventing the creation of a normal Palestinian state. The American way out of it is a two-state solution whose small print shall be a demilitarized Palestine guaranteed by a de facto US-Israeli alliance.

In a study published recently by the Tel Aviv University think tank IISS, two experts assessed that the American support for Israel in the present war 'has been unprecedented' in terms of diplomatic support, ongoing military assistance and strategic support, but also in growing criticism of Israel's conduct and increasing efforts to shape the post-war situation. It adds that the predominantly Jewish community (in the US) and particularly its younger members 'are distancing themselves from Israel' and the same can be said of domestic attitudes in Israel.

The respective requirements of the affected or interested parties to this long-standing dispute, in the light of the experience of 7 October, can be summed up thus:

(a) Palestinians: Recognition of their existence as a state along with rights as a state under international law and in terms of the Palestinian Non-Paper of 12.06.2002
(b) Israel: Retention of the acquired territory. 'The Palestinians would be given all the powers to govern themselves but

none of the powers that could threaten Israel. Put simply, the solution is self-government for the Palestinians with vital security powers retained by Israel.'

(c) United States: A two-state solution with a demilitarized Gaza, a Saudi normalization with Israel, a role for the moderate Arab countries in rebuilding Gaza, and in keeping Iran isolated.

In the last week of February, Thomas Friedman wrote about 'the increasingly rapid erosion of Israel's standing among friendly nations', and that 'if Biden is not careful, America's global standing will plummet right along with Israel's.'

(d) Arab states: A revitalized Palestinian state, devoid of radical elements after the experience of the Arab Spring, and benefiting from the experience of Egypt and Jordan and of the states party to the Abraham Accords. May not be averse to American suggestions of an Arab Mandate.

One needs to be an optimist, even a 'panglossian', to consider these realizable!

Chapter 17

A Civilizational Existential Threat

On 24 June 2020, the UN Secretary-General António Guterres noted in a virtual meeting of the United Nations Security Council that the Israeli-Palestinian conflict is at a 'watershed moment' and that Israeli plans to annex parts of the West Bank have alarmed the Palestinians, many Israelis and the international community. Such annexation would be 'a most serious violation of international law'.[97] He called upon the Israeli government to abandon its annexation plans and asked the Middle East Quartet (the United States, Russia, the European Union and the UN) to resume its mandated mediatory role.

A VIOLATION

The UN Secretary-General's alarm has been sounded in the context of the Israeli Prime Minister Benjamin Netanyahu's reported plan to annex on 1 July around 30 per cent of the Occupied West Bank. This will include annexation of all the existing (post-1967) settlements in addition to areas surrounding them and access roads. This, from published accounts, has the approval of the Trump Administration.

Under international law, annexation is forcible acquisition of

---

[97]Guterres, Antonio, 'Secretary-General's Virtual Briefing to the Security Council on the Situation in the Middle East, including the Question of Palestine', *United Nations.org*, 24 June 2020, https://tinyurl.com/ycxu5k3f. Accessed on 25 September 2025.

territory by one state at the expense of another state. According to Prof. Nathaniel A Berman of Brown University, US, such an act, even if sanctified by Israeli law, is illegal under international law and would violate the universally acknowledged principle of the 'inadmissibility of the acquisition of territory by force'. This, according to him, is the accepted position of all international legal bodies including the International Court of Justice.

The same position has been taken by the Office of the High Commissioner for Human Rights (UN Human Rights). In a statement on 16 June, it described the annexation of an occupied territory as a serious violation of the Charter of the United Nations and the Geneva Conventions and contrary to the fundamental rule, affirmed many times by the UN Security Council and the General Assembly that acquisition of territory through war or by force is inadmissible. It pointed out that the 53-year-old Israeli occupation is a source of profound human rights violations of the Palestinian people and stated:

> These human right violations would only intensify after annexation. What would be left of the West Bank would be Palestinian Bantustan, islands of disconnected land completely surrounded by Israel and with no territorial connection with the outside world. Israel has recently promised that it will maintain permanent security control between the Mediterranean and the Jordan River. Thus, the morning after the annexation would be the crystallisation of an already unjust reality: two peoples living in the same space, ruled by the same state, but with profoundly unequal rights. This is a vision of a 21st century apartheid.[98]

---

[98]Office of the High Commissioner, 'Israeli annexation of parts of the Palestinian West Bank would break international law—UN experts call on the international community to ensure accountability', United Nations Human Rights, 16 June 2020, https://tinyurl.com/y4w4b5tu. Accessed on 19 September 2025.

The statement concludes that despite the dismal record of Israel's past violation of international law, 'accountability and an end to impunity must become an immediate priority for the international community.'[99]

THE ISRAELI PULSE

Despite Mr Netanyahu's bravado, an opinion poll conducted in March last year by the Israeli newspaper *Haaretz* showed that while 28 per cent of the Israelis opposed annexation, 11 per cent supported full annexation with political rights for the Palestinians, and 16 per cent full annexation with no political rights for Palestinians. In addition, 15 per cent were for partial annexation and 30 per cent expressed no views.

An interesting and unprecedented entrant in the debate is an opinion article titled 'It's either Annexation or Normalization', published in an Israeli newspaper, *Yediot Ahronot*, and written in Hebrew by the United Arab Emirates ambassador in Washington. It urged the Israeli government to desist from the contemplated move.

What would be the consequences of such a move? Would Palestinians living in annexed areas, and owning around 23 per cent of its land, retain their private property? Would they be enshrined in a legal framework of a two-class population divided by ethnicity and given Israeli residency as a category of 'subjects' of the annexing entity? Would they be on par with Israeli Arabs of Palestinian origin (Muslim, Christian and Druze) who together constitute about 20 per cent of Israel's population? Above all, will it take away from Palestinians the right to have their own state under the right of national self-determination recognized times without number by the international community?

---

[99]Ibid.

Would there be demographic consequences? Israel, in the words of its former Prime Minister Ben Gurion, by its foundational proclamations, 'is not only a Jewish state, where the majority of the inhabitants are Jews, but a state for all Jews, wherever they are, and for every Jew who wants to be here. [...] This right is inherent in his being a Jew.'[100] Its official ideology of Zionism (somewhat analogous to other doctrines of strident nationalism of the 20th century) was described much earlier by Vladimir Jabotinsky as 'a colonizing adventure and therefore it stands or falls by the question of armed force.'[101]

Ever since the war of June 1967, the Israeli effort has been to procrastinate a settlement and change ground realities. Israel today is a member of the international community and contributes to international cooperation. It has succeeded in normalizing its relations with a wide range of countries. A concomitant of this is the observance of globally accepted norms of state conduct. A reluctance to do this is premised on the support of 'powerful friends' and imperatives of geopolitics. Must this necessarily have permanence? The record of Palestinian resistance and of protest movements the world over show that injustice and denial of rights have no permanence and, as Jean Jacques Rousseau said a long time back, 'the strongest is never strong enough to be always master unless he transforms his power into right, and obedience into duty.'

FOR NEW DELHI

India has a substantive relationship, reaching strategic dimensions, with Israel. It is mutually beneficial. India's amity with the

---

[100]Savir, Yabuda, 'The Definition of a Jew under Israel's Law of Return', *SMU Law Review*, Vol. 17, No. 1, 1963, pp. 123–133, https://tinyurl.com/pmu4nebe. Accessed on 19 September 2025.

[101]Brenner, Lenni, 'Founding Principles of Zionist Revisionism', *The Iron Wall*, Zed Books, London, 1984.

Palestinian people, and its principled support to their cause, predates India's own independence. On the global stage, we have invariably supported the UN Security Council and General Assembly resolutions supportive of the Palestinians.

At this critical juncture, and now that we are back on the Horse Shoe Table, would we support an annexation in contravention of international legality and of our own commitments?

Chapter 18

The Voice of a Gaza under Occupation

While the conflict rages in Gaza amidst allegations and counter-allegations, and in the midst of unabashed American partiality, it is relevant to recall what the senior leader of Hamas, Mousa Abu Marzouk, told *The New Yorker* magazine (13 October 2023) about the political approach: 'We rolled down all of the pathways to get some of our rights—not all of them. We knocked on the door of reconciliation and we weren't allowed in. We knocked on the door of elections and we were deprived of them. We knocked on the door of a political document for the whole world—we said, "We want peace, but give us some of our rights"—but they didn't let us in.' He added, 'We tried every path. We didn't find one political path to take us out of this morass and free us from occupation. [...] We spoke to the Americans, Europeans and all of the people in order to achieve the Palestinian people's rights, without any benefit. Nothing has been achieved towards the idea of two states, from 1948 until today. We are a people under occupation.'[102]

Abu Marzouk added that in earlier conflicts, the Israelis waged wars outside their borders: 'This is the first time that the Palestinians are crossing the borders and fighting in their

[102]Rasgon, Adam, and David D. Kirkpatrick, 'What Was Hamas Thinking', *The New Yorker*, 13 October 2023, https://tinyurl.com/bdftjvjw. Accessed on 24 September 2025.

historic land.'[103] The conflict has shattered the aura of invincibility.

TEL AVIV'S RESPONSE

The Israeli response to the Hamas attack has been to order the evacuation of the northern half of Gaza, to enforce it by a blockade, by the cutting off of food, water and electricity, as also by the massing of 300,000 troops on Gaza's border. The objective presumably is to occupy the northern zone and expand space for new settlements. The Palestinians see it as such and recall the manner in which the state of Israel came into existence on 14 May 1948, when 656,000 Arab[104] inhabitants of the Mandate Territory of Palestine were made to flee by what the historian Paul Johnson called in his book, *History of the Jews*, 'the scientific use of terror to break the will of liberal rulers.' Palestinians were thus made to pay for the genocide of Jews in Europe which was committed by Germans, not Arabs.

The ideological motivation, particularly of the present Israeli leadership, should not be overlooked either. It has repeatedly equated the Palestinians with the Nazis who should be eliminated. This is a reiteration of what Vladimir Jabotinsky, a respected predecessor of right-wing Zionism said in 1923: Zionism 'is a colonizing adventure and therefore it stands or falls by the question of armed force.'[105] He predicted that the Palestinian will not leave his land unless confronted 'by a wall of Jewish bayonets so that a new race, proud, generous and cruel, shall arise.'

The reality of this perception has been reinforced by decades of connivance by world powers. Innumerable

[103]Ibid.

[104]Toynbee, A.J., 'Foreword', *The Palestine Diary, 1914-1945*, by Robert John and Sami Hadawi, New World Press, New York, 1970.

[105]Jabotinsky, Vladimir, https://tinyurl.com/yckbs37v. Accessed on 25 September 2025.

United Nations Security Council (UNSC) resolutions have remained unimplemented. Each reiterated the earlier ones and some even indicated new goalposts; each sought to explain away the guilt of the culprits. Resolution 2334 of December 2016, for instance, outlawed all settlement activity and reiterated the desirability of implementing the two-state solution.

A departure from the UNSC route was attempted in September 2020 by the Abraham Accords seeking, piously, to 'end radicalization and conflict' while ignoring the causes of both. An expectation of expanding the ambit of both has not materialized.

NO MORE INVINCIBLE

Israel's objectives for the Gaza operation have been officially identified with precision: toppling Hamas and destroying its military capabilities; eliminating the threat of terrorism emanating from the Gaza strip; exerting maximum pressure to find a solution to the hostage issue; and defending the borders of the state and its citizens. These would require going into Gaza. Informed Arab columnists like Abdel Bari Atwan are of the opinion that the most recent fighting has deprived Israel of its two most effective weapons: its scariness and its deterrent power. Such a move, he says, would be more far-reaching than Ehud Olmert's foray and Ariel Sharon's venture.

The response of the United States and some of its allies to the present crisis raises the question of motivation. Did they know more about the chink in Israel's armour? Did they apprehend the implications of conflict going beyond Gaza and its adverse impact on Israel?

PERTINENT QUESTIONS

The prognosis of Thomas L. Friedman in *The New York Times* article of 16 October 2023 sheds light on the prospects:

> If Israel goes into Gaza now, it will blow up the Abraham Accords, further destabilize two of America's most important allies (Egypt and Jordan) and make normalization with Saudi Arabia impossible—huge strategic setbacks. It will also enable Hamas to really fire up the West Bank and get a shepherd's war going there between Jewish settlers and Palestinians. Altogether, it will play directly into Iran's strategy of sucking Israel into imperial overstretch and in that way weakening the Jewish democracy from within.[106]

Friedman adds:

> While Biden is right to support Israel, he must get clear answers from Netanyahu now, before it's too late: Once Israel topples Hamas, who will govern Gaza? If Israel intends to govern Gaza, will it pay for the rebuilding of the infrastructure that it is destroying? And if not, who will? How long does Israel intend to allow the humanitarian crisis to unfold in southern Gaza? Does Israel plan to build settlements in Gaza? Does Israel respect Gaza's borders? Does it have a plan to help rebuild the Palestinian Authority in the West Bank?[107]

US President Joe Biden was emphatic in his condemnation of Hamas for the responsibility of the hospital attack. Its timing is yet to be established and Professor Anthony H. Cordesman of the Center for Strategic and International Studies is of the opinion that the only way to convince those who do not take sides is to establish some form of international investigation that is led by nations or individuals who are credible.

---

[106]Friedman, Thomas L., 'Why a Gaza Invasion and 'Once and for All' Thinking Are Wrong for Israel', *The New York Times*, 16 October 2023, https://tinyurl.com/2f5ecwr4. Accessed on 25 September 2025.
[107]Ibid.

Clearly, there may be merit in Abu Marzouk's claim. Hasty resort to partiality may not be the option.

This article was originally published in The Hindu *on 27 October 2023, under the headline 'The voice of a Gaza under occupation'.*

Chapter 19

The Arab World and the Elusive Two-State Solution

Words have meanings that are used and misused. A few weeks ago, someone with evident limitations fulminated against a category of faiths depicted as 'Abrahamic'. Around the same time, the global media gleefully proclaimed the newly minted 'Abraham Accords' to describe a happening of political significance. Both expressions sought to trace it to the proper name, Abraham, a patriarchal entity who flourished in the second millennium BCE, who is revered by three religions, Judaism, Christianity and Islam, and whose followers today account for a little over 55 per cent of the world's population. Mention is also made alongside of a group of languages as Semitic: principally Arabic, Hebrew, Amharic and Aramaic.

LANGUAGE AS FULCRUM

Till the end of World War I, most of the Arabic-speaking lands of West Asia and North Africa were ruled directly or indirectly by the Ottoman Empire. Today, thanks to geopolitical cartography, they constitute the 'Arab World' whose 22 members are members of the UN. The point of commonality is the language.

The seeds of Arab nationalism were sown in the 19th century. The classic work of George Antonius, published in 1938, records the origins: 'It was at a secret gathering of the certain members of the Syrian Scientific Society that the Arab national movement may be said to have uttered its first cry.'[108] A poem by one of its members gave it the battle cry: Arise, ye Arabs, and awake! The poem, viewed as seditious by the Ottoman rulers, did much to foster the national movement in its infancy.

A CRITIQUE

In 1945 and reportedly on British prompting, the League of Arab States was formed to 'draw closer the relations between member states and co-ordinate their political activities with the aim of realizing a close collaboration between them, to safeguard their independence and sovereignty, and to consider in a general way the affairs and interests of the Arab countries.'[109] It has achieved none of its objectives and its hopes have been 'worn down to disillusion and cynicism' emanating from what Bassam Tibi has called 'the duality of words and deeds'.

The critique of mystifications of Arab nationalism was a promise; but the promise of getting light at the end of the tunnel did not bear the expected results. This was attributed by a UNDP Human Development Report many years ago to deficits of knowledge, freedom and empowerment of women. Thus, absence of participatory governance and its institutions, disregard for individual freedoms, and the prevalence of one-person rule resulted in what Abdallah Laroui characterized as 'living in infra-historical rhythm'[110]. Admittedly, sectional, though uneven, progress was made, but as the experience of the Arab

[108]Antonius, George, *The Arab Awakening: The Story of the Arab National Movement*, H. Hamilton, London, 1938.

[109]The Avalon Project, 'Pact of the League of Arab States, March 22, 1945', Yale Law School, https://tinyurl.com/rjefks86. Accessed on 19 September 2025.

[110]Ansari, M. Hamid, 'A Century of Turmoil in Western Asia: Some Pitfalls of Nationalism', *Contemporary Review of the Middle East*, Vol. 1, No. 4, 2015, https://tinyurl.com/vuw48cu2. Accessed on 19 September 2025.

Uprising of 2011 showed, deep disagreements prevented the emergence of an Arab order and its impact on 'Arab unity'. It was most evident in their responses to regional and global problems.

THE PALESTINE ISSUE

The one problem on which Arab states professed unity of opinion, but not necessarily of approach, related to Palestine and to the demand for a Palestinian state. After multiple resorts to war and popular uprisings, the tenacity of Israel and its American backers forced the Arab states and their international supporters to accept the Camp David and Oslo Accords and finally the Saudi-sponsored 2002 Arab Peace Initiative. It involved a de facto recognition of Israel and the latter accepted it with 14 reservations.

The truth behind this Saudi initiative has now been made public in a series of television interviews on Al-Arabiya channel on 5 October by the former Saudi ambassador to the United States and later intelligence chief, Prince Bandar Bin Sultan. It is candid and revealing and sheds much light on the Saudi suspicion of the Palestine Liberation Organisation (PLO) leadership, beginning but not ending with Yasser Arafat.

The ostensible reason for this, according to some Arab-American commentators, is a 'perceived threat from Iran, the spread of regional terrorism and the rise of Islamism.' The take-off occasion, according to them, was the conference in Warsaw in February 2019 that was hailed by Israel's Prime Minister Netanyahu as 'a breakthrough in Arab-Israeli relations'. This could be seen as a stage in the success of Israel's grand strategy candidly spelt out in Yossi Alpher's 2015 book, *Periphery*, aimed to outflank the hostile core that surrounds it, and gain the major political-security goal of countering Arab hostility through relations with alternate regional powers and potential allies. It has been furthered by post-2011 developments in individual Arab countries and the aura bestowed on 'political Islam' or Islamism, presented by its protagonists such as Fahmy Howeidy, who argued that Arab nationalism is a stage towards greater Islamic unity.

PUBLIC OPINION VS POLICY

Do these failures to jolt the system at the individual-country and regional levels have an impact on perceptions of the Palestinian problem? The Arab Center Washington DC and its *Arab Opinion Index* for 2019–20 published last week concluded that 79 per cent of the respondents felt 'the Palestinian cause concerns all Arabs and not the Palestinian people alone'[111]. This figure in 2012–13 was 84 per cent. It is thus difficult not to conclude that opinion at the public/respondent level is not in step with official policy orientation on this question. Does this in any manner further the Palestinian cause, more so because the direction of Israeli policy premised on incremental creation of facts on the ground, together with furtherance of practical cooperation with individual Arab countries, would inevitably result in de facto annexation of most parts of the West Bank even if a formal annexation is deferred?

A WAY OUT

The PLO leadership has been left high and dry even if not yet disowned by its own people. Would the new situation propel it to recraft its policies? The promised two-state solution is nowhere in sight except for some variants of Bantustans. Would it not be better to explore a one-state solution even if it involves a South Africa-like apartheid that would sooner or later prick the conscience of world opinion and their governments and allow a

[111]Arab Center for Research and Policy Studies, https://tinyurl.com/48kbvk2y. Accessed on 25 September 2025.

Palestinian-Mandela to use Gandhian principles to seek justice?

Therefore, the Arab World in a geopolitical sense no longer exists. It will retain its focus on linguistic homogeneity and attendant cultural glory. As for the Palestinians and in the event of hard tactical options being forsaken, they might even explore the creation of a Palestinian point of lamentation, a 'wailing wall', hoping that divine justice would eventually be forthcoming as has been with their Abrahamic cousins.

This article was originally published in The Hindu *on 14 October 2020, under the headline 'The Arab World and the elusive two-state solution'.*

Chapter 20

Follies in a Haunted Battleground

Geography dictates geopolitics but is often interpreted varyingly. This has been true of Afghanistan in modern times. Before 1880, its boundaries were demographic rather than territorial and as a political entity it began to emerge when the empires of the Safavids in the west and Moghuls in the east declined rapidly. Until then, it was nominally a monarchy but in reality a military aristocracy, and the death of a ruler was always followed by civil wars.

In the 1880s, Amir Abdur Rahman Khan cautioned his country against Tsarist inroads. In the Anglo-Russian Convention of 1907, the two imperial powers committed themselves not to undertake change in the political status of Afghanistan. In 1953, the Joint Chiefs of Staff in Washington concluded that 'Afghanistan is of little or no strategic importance to the United States' and that 'it would be desirable to remain neutral because otherwise it might be overrun as an avenue to the Indian subcontinent.' In October 1954, Secretary of State Dulles told a high-ranking Afghan emissary that 'instead of asking for arms, Afghanistan should settle the Pashtunistan dispute with Pakistan.'[112]

A quarter of a century later and following the establishment of a Soviet-backed government in Kabul, national security advisor Brzezinski advised President Carter to choose between punitive, coercive or deterrent courses of retaliatory action 'to maintain

[112]Statement of Admiral Arthur W. Radford, Chairman of the US Joint Chiefs of Staff.

credibility in Moscow'. A decision was then taken in June 1979 to establish ties with Afghan dissident leaders in Pakistan and offer aid to them. This, in turn, led to Moscow's direct armed intervention on 27 December 1979.

In response, a trilateral alliance of the United States, Pakistan and Saudi Arabia emerged to render assistance to the Mujahideen groups through an 'arms pipeline' controlled by the Afghan Bureau of the ISI. The latter also decided on the allocation of funds made available principally by Saudi Arabia to different groups and coordinated with the CIA and the Saudi intelligence organization headed by Prince Turki Al Faisal, who has recently given a candid account of it.

CARTER'S GOAL

Carter's aim, according to Turki, 'was to embarrass the Soviet Union and make the cost of occupation of Afghanistan as high as possible…the war in Afghanistan was more a political and military failure than a conventional military defeat for the Soviet Union. […] In a military sense it failed to subdue the Mujahideen but it never suffered a defeat in battle.' More details of the process were given many years earlier in Artyom Borovik's *Hidden War* that shed much light on the Soviet conduct of the war and on the morale of its armed forces.

In 1982, Brezhnev posed a question to Prime Minister Indira Gandhi: 'Show me a way to get out of Afghanistan'; her response was laconic: 'the way out is the same as the way in.'[113] A face-saving formula, however, took time to emerge since Washington showed no haste and the Soviet withdrawal was thus completed only in February 1989.

[113]Aiyar, Mani Shankar, 'When Brezhnev Pleased with Indira Gandhi', *The Indian Express*, 18 June 2016, https://tinyurl.com/ycxcsjs9. Accessed on 25 September 2025.

In August 1919, the Treaty of Rawalpindi recognized Afghanistan as a fully sovereign state and the Amir in turn recognized the Durand Line and agreed to forego the British subsidy. In July 1931, king Nadir Shah announced a policy of neutrality. In July 1949, the Afghan National Assembly passed a resolution repudiating all previous treaties and agreements with the British before the birth of Pakistan and rejected the Durand Line as the international frontier.

Decades later, Pakistan's perceptions changed after the collapse of the PDPA regime in the wake of the Soviet withdrawal and the seven-party Mujahideen government was installed and recognized by many Western states. New Delhi then took the view that our diplomatic mission in Kabul should continue and so should our economic assistance and help in the area of public health. It was also decided that we 'should contact with leaders of all groups and remain in touch with them so that eventually India could deal with whosoever came to power.'[114]

AN IDEA TO PURSUE

Then and later, the idea of an externally guaranteed institutionalized neutrality was aired but not welcomed by the Mujahideen, and even later, President Karzai was not receptive when the word was 'used carelessly' by the UN Special Representative Kai Eide in the context of Afghanistan's future international status. On the other hand, and in more recent times, the idea has been aired from time to time (including by two from India) as a possible remedy for minimizing or ending competition between powers, and to prevent Afghanistan from becoming a geopolitical pivot of competing powers and a source of extremism and terrorism.

---

[114]Bhattacharjee, Kallol, *The Great Game in Afghanistan, Rajiv Gandhi, General Zia and the Unending War*, HarperCollins, Noida, India, 2017.

An American scholar Audrey Cronin studied in 2016 recent cases of 'Neutralization as a Sustainable Approach' and, in relation to Afghanistan, opined that such an approach could be negotiated by the US, China, Iran, Russia, Saudi Arabia, Central Asian republics and NATO, adding that the question of the Durand Line would need to be addressed during negotiations.

In December 2003, two Indian commentators opined that the way out of the morass would be to replace Afghanistan in its traditional mode of neutrality, for which two requirements were essential: (a) the Afghans themselves must declare unequivocally that they would follow strict neutrality in their relations with external powers, and (b) outside powers must commit themselves to respect Afghanistan's neutrality. In other words, external powers must subscribe to a multilateral declaration not to interfere in the internal affairs of Afghanistan, together with an obligation on Afghanistan not to seek outside intervention in its internal situation.

A suggestion of 'neutralization' as a concept and as a realizable goal has to be thought through on grounds of principle and of practicality. In the first place, would there be an ideological constraint from the viewpoint of the present-day Taliban? None have been mentioned and should not be presumed. Available accounts of the Doha talks suggest that both former president Ashraf Ghani and the US Special Envoy Khalilzad mentioned 'neutral and non-aligned Afghanistan post-peace settlement Afghanistan'[115] in the discussions and were not contradicted in terms of Islamic ideology as viewed by the Taliban. It is on record that Afghan governments practised neutralism (military non-alignment) since King Nadir Shah's pronouncement in 1931—in

[115]Asey, Tamim, 'Rebooting neutrality in Afghan foreign policy—A framework for global and regional engagement on Afghanistan post-US and NATO withdrawal', *Atlantic Council*, 29 April 2021, https://tinyurl.com/59dccv5s. Accessed on 29 September 2025.

World War II and in the India-Pakistan wars of 1965 and 1971 and the Kargil wars. In the foreseeable future and given domestic cohesion, the likelihood of the Taliban leadership departing from it on ideological or practical grounds does not seem to arise.

PRACTICALITY

This leaves the factor of practicality that is to be tested on the regime's immediate and foreseeable future requirements: recognition, de-freezing of assets, immediate food aid, and longer-term bilateral and multilateral economic assistance to replace what was given bilaterally for other considerations.

The essential ingredients of such neutralization would be (a) a formal Afghan declaration in constitutional terms, (b) a legally binding declaration by each and every immediate and proximate neighbour, (c) a UN Security Council declaration calling on the P5 and interested powers to refrain from any form of power politics in Afghanistan, and (d) a UN General Assembly resolution recognizing Afghanistan as a neutral state.

On the Durand Line, and while nothing has been formally proposed, the solution would seem to lie in a creative approach with some form of a formal but soft border that would accommodate the area's history, geography and demography. In this context, an observation by the former Pakistan foreign secretary Riaz Mohammad Khan is of relevance: 'It would be as futile for Pakistan to push Kabul for formal recognition of the Durand Line as it is for Kabul to reopen this issue whose parameters it has never been able to define. Kabul should continue to respect the Durand Line as the functional border, which for Pakistan remains the historical and legal border.'[116]

---

[116]Khan, Riaz Mohammad, *Afghanistan and Pakistan: Conflict, Extremism, and Resistance to Modernity*, Oxford University Press, New Delhi, 2011, p. 338.

Given the ground situation today, and Afghanistan's dire need for accommodation with the external powers, aid givers and economic assistance, the situation is ripe for political adjustment of its basic perceptions, more so because it can benefit, not harm, the country and allow friendly countries to render assistance without constraints of competition and power politics.

In futile efforts, great powers have tried and failed to dominate the world through Afghanistan, and left death and misery in its wake. Sanity would suggest a wiser approach.

This article was originally published in The Hindu *on 23 November 2021, under the headline 'Reversing follies in a haunted battleground'.*

Chapter 21

Diplomacy, with a Change in Terms of Reference

Mediation is rarely a spontaneous act; more often than not, it is preceded by quiet efforts to seek a meeting point between differing viewpoints of individuals or organizations. It figures in Article 33 of the United Nations Charter among means of 'Pacific Settlement of Disputes'. But in legal terms, it is different from Good Offices and Arbitration.

A good instance of this was recently witnessed on the global stage. The question of motivation can be debated. In a joint statement on 10 March 2023, Iran, Saudi Arabia and China (sitting at a table in the shape of an isosceles triangle) announced that an agreement had been reached between the Kingdom of Saudi Arabia and the Islamic Republic of Iran covering a resumption of diplomatic relations between them and a re-opening of their embassies and missions within a period not exceeding two months. The agreement affirmed their respect for the sovereignty of states and non-interference in the internal affairs of states, and said that the ministers of foreign affairs of both countries would meet to implement this, arrange for the return of their ambassadors, and discuss means of enhancing bilateral relations. Iranian National Security Adviser Ali Shamkhani (who is seen in the official photograph of the ceremony) is from the Office of the Supreme Leader in Iran and lends credibility to the accord.

A commentary in an Iranian newspaper on 11 March 2023

depicted the event as 'One agreement and seven achievements'[117]; it listed the latter as Tehran's willingness to engage in dialogue; failure of US effort to isolate Iran; strengthening of the alliance of Islamic countries; failure of Israeli efforts against this agreement; failure of US effort to show the Iranian public that it had no choice but to agree to the JCPOA with America; Beijing's successful entry in West Asian relations; and failure of dreams of 'regime change'.

AMERICAN AND ISRAELI REACTIONS

Later that month—and writing with a good deal of caution—a Chinese academic observed in the *Global Times* that 'China's diplomacy as a major power is just getting started' and may even result in some marked changes in the regional situation.

US reactions, apart from unconcealed surprise, reflected the change in terms of reference in international diplomacy. Equally surprised was Israel, the other major player in the region, which saw it as a fatal blow to the effort to build a regional coalition against Iran. One commentator said: 'China brought Saudi Arabia together with Iran at a time when Israel had hoped that the United States would bring it together with Saudi Arabia.' Henry Kissinger told David Ignatius of *The Washington Post*, 'I see it as a substantial change in the strategic situation in the Middle East. The Saudis are now balancing their security by playing off the US against China.'[118]

Aaron Miller, who served for long as a State Department adviser on Middle East, said the development 'demonstrates that [the] US's influence and credibility in the region has [have]

---

[117]Sarfi, Mohammad, 'One agreement and seven achievements', *Tehran Times*, 11 March 2023, https://tinyurl.com/mwdx4he7. Accessed on 25 November 2025.

[118]Ignatius, David, 'How China is heralding the beginnings of a multipolar Middle East', *The Washington Post*, 16 March 2023, https://tinyurl.com/cabpccwb. Accessed on 22 November 2025.

diminished and a new sort of international regional alignment is taking place which has empowered and given both Russia and China newfound influence and status.'

The backdrop to the event is noteworthy. Bilateral efforts have been underway since early 2016 to ease tensions that had developed specifically between Tehran, Riyadh and Abu Dhabi, and generally within the Gulf Cooperation Council (GCC) in relation to Yemen and Syria. The Emir of Kuwait and the Sultan of Oman initiated steps that were responded to by Iran. Talks were also held in Baghdad and during Iranian President Ebrahim Raisi's visit to China in February. All concerned were worried about the attacks on shipping and energy facilities in the Kingdom of Saudi Arabia (KSA) and the United Arab Emirates, and the long-term implications of the regional conflicts that were underway. These together 'brought home the risks of being on the front line of confrontation.'

The official visit by China's President Xi Jinping to Saudi Arabia in December 2022 also saw him attending the first China-Arab States Summit and the China-GCC Summit. The theme of his address was 'Building on Past Achievements and Jointly Creating a Brighter Future of China-GCC Relations'. China and the GCC, he stressed, should be partners for common security: China will continue to firmly support GCC countries in safeguarding their security, and support the efforts by countries of the region to resolve differences through dialogue and consultations and to build a Gulf security architecture. China, he said, 'welcomes the participation of GCC countries in the Global Security Initiative (GSI) in a joint effort to uphold regional peace and stability.'

The speech laid stress on five priority areas: energy cooperation; finance and investment cooperation; innovation, science and technology; aerospace cooperation; and Chinese language and cultural cooperation. An Action Plan for 2023–27 was agreed upon. A comprehensive Strategic Partnership Agreement with specific agreements and some memoranda of understanding were also signed. It said the two supported 'each other's core interests'. The Chinese side 'commended the efforts made' by the Kingdom to serve Chinese Haj and Umrah pilgrims. The statement stressed the importance of deepening cooperation with regard to the Belt and Road Initiative (BRI) and on attracting Chinese expertise in Saudi megaprojects. The two sides signed 'a harmonizing plan' between the KSA's Vision 2030 and the BRI. It is reported that a China-GCC summit in Beijing was being scheduled.

THE INDIAN STAND

India's reaction to this development has been restrained. Apart from historical linkages, the region is in India's proximate neighbourhood and within its security parameters. It is the principal source of hydrocarbon imports, and increasingly of investments. It is also an important destination for workforce exports apart from being a major trading partner, including projects. The official policy has focused on bilateral relations and avoidance of involvement in bilateral and regional disputes. Given these priorities, India has consciously refrained from speculative ventures in alternate security architecture apart from supporting cooperative security and freedom of waterways and of navigation. The region should not be viewed in competition with China without the latter's economic and military capacity, nor should India consider itself a surrogate for those who have been outplayed, at least for the moment, in power games for transitory affection.

This article was originally published in The Hindu *on 17 April 2023, under the headline 'Diplomacy, with a change in terms of reference'.*

Chapter 22

Saudi Arabia, Iran and the Possibilities of Détente

Individuals and human collectives have memories and time spans. The two do not converge but at times overlap. The latter are infrequent yet meaningful. Prudence, if not wisdom, lies in using them. One such occasion betides the Gulf region at this juncture.

The Persian Gulf is a nearly 990-kilometre-long body of water that separates Iran from the Arabian Peninsula. Seven member states of the United Nations lay claim to washing their hands or feet in its waters. At its narrowest point, in the Strait of Hormuz, it is only 54 km wide and the shipping lanes are just 3 km wide in each direction. They are critical to the transportation of crude oil and LNG to global markets.

For over a century till the early 1970s, the Persian Gulf was a British lake. The imperial withdrawal propelled the United States to step in as the guarantor of the sub-region with its Twin-Pillars (Iran-Saudi Arabia) policy. An abortive effort was also made by Oman through the Muscat Conference in November 1976; it floundered on the obstinacy of Baathist Iraq. Bilateral efforts were also made by King Faisal of Saudi Arabia and the Shah of Iran; King Faisal initiated his Islamic solidarity policy in 1964 and visited Iran in December 1965; in 1966, Saudi Defence Minister Sultan bin Abdulaziz described the Iranian-Saudi friendship as a perfect example of Islamic brotherhood and neighbourly relations; the two states were also active members of the Five Power 'Safari Club' for intelligence sharing.

IMPACT OF UNREST

The Iranian Revolution of 1978–79 disturbed the strategic balance in the region and put an end to efforts to develop a regional consensus on security issues. Over the next decade, and particularly during the period of the Iraq-Iran war, the Gulf monarchies and their Western supporters put an effort to destabilize and wish away the revolutionary regime. The formation of the Gulf Cooperation Council (GCC) in 1981 was part of the effort to reassure the Gulf sheikhdoms. The end of the war and the cooling of tensions allowed saner perceptions to emerge. The Saudi Arabian Foreign Minister, among others, spelt these out in the Manama Dialogue in December 2004. In 1996, Iranian President Mohammad Khatami told the Saudi Defence Minister that a defence pact would be mutually beneficial. Crown Prince Abdullah attended the Islamic Summit conference in Tehran on 9–11 December 1997. This was seen in Tehran as 'a good beginning for removing misunderstandings'. Subsequent developments in the region relating to Syria and the Hezbollah on the one side and the Saudi intervention in Yemen on the other pushed back, even reversed, the developing perceptions in Riyadh.

Yemen in particular has been critical to Saudi perceptions of national security. The clash of viewpoints dates back to the 1930s when King Abdulaziz ibn Saud was expanding the boundaries of the Kingdom of Najd to incorporate the western and southern parts of the Arabian Peninsula. Conflict developed over the southern region of Najran and resulted in a Saudi military victory and the Treaty of 1934. This maintained peace till the Egyptian Revolution and Gamal Abdel Nasser's 'intoxicating blend of nationalism and radicalism' that set the region alight. It led to the Yemeni coup of 1962, the Egyptian military intervention in Yemen and the souring of Saudi-Egyptian relations that lasted till the Arab-Israeli War of 1967. This suited the interests of the United States; military assistance programmes and the stationing of US troops during the Kuwait War of 1990 followed. The Trump era and the jettisoning of the Joint Comprehensive Plan of Action witnessed a qualitative strengthening of ties between them.

THE KEY ISSUES

The last few years have witnessed geopolitical tensions in the Gulf littoral. Most states have been affected adversely by the historically low oil prices and by Covid-19. The GCC has become inoperative with the focus on the boycott of Qatar that is now being reversed. There are new tensions between the United Arab Emirates (UAE) and Saudi Arabia. Riyadh's access to the Oval Office in Washington is now not what it was in the Donald Trump era. The Abraham Accords between Israel, the UAE and Bahrain have qualitatively influenced the Arab-Israeli calculus in the Persian Gulf states and in the wider Arab world.

More recently, the US's decision to withdraw forces from Afghanistan and reduce commitments in Iraq has been the subject of discussions on policy options among knowledgeable observers in Washington. One expert has observed that 'on balance, the American ground-force base in Kuwait, the Fifth Fleet naval base in Bahrain, [the] Al Udeid Air Base in Qatar, Al Dhafra Air Base in the UAE and the access arrangements in Oman provide the US with a politically and financially sustainable military presence'[119] in the region. Another view is that 'the post-Covid-19 environment is going to be unfriendly to Saudi Arabia perhaps more than to

[119]Gause, F.G., 'Should We Stay or Should We Go? The United States and the Middle East', *Survival*, *61*(5), 7–24, 2019, https://tinyurl.com/ycky25k2. Accessed on 22 November 2025.

any other leading power in the Gulf.' The Saudi failure to subdue the Houthis and to close the Yemen conflict on their terms has become a source of concern. The US's inability to subdue Iran on its terms has also become evident. Others have drawn attention to the Saudi Crown Prince's remark in April that his country wants good relations with Iran and to the Iranian reaction of welcoming it. It is evident that policy options are being explored.

SECURITY IS THE CONCERN

The impact of these recent developments in Saudi Arabia-Iran relations needs to be assessed in this context. The effort to impart a sectarian orientation to the divide does not seem to hold. Their primary concern is security in the Gulf littoral and the security of the waterway for the transportation of their hydrocarbon exports.

In January 1987, the then US Secretary of State said the Gulf had become 'critical to the economic health of the West'. A good part of the rest of the world can be justifiably added to it.

For this to be given practical shape, its essential ingredients would need to be freedom of access to, and outlet from, Gulf waters through the Strait of Hormuz; freedom of commercial shipping in international waters in the Persian Gulf; prevention of conflict that may impinge on the freedom of trade and shipping; freedom to all states of the Gulf littoral to exploit their hydrocarbons and other natural resources and export them; ensure conditions of peace and stability in the individual littoral states, and ensure that regional or extra-regional conditions do not impinge on any of these considerations.

Could the achievement of such an arrangement, or a part of it, be the beginning of a much desired and reassuring development? Over time, it may address itself to bring forth answers to questions such as security for whom, by whom, against whom.

The pronouncements from Riyadh and Tehran do tend

to suggest an inclination to be supportive of some of these suggestions. This is to be welcomed since, from an Indian viewpoint, the requirement is and will continue to be stability in the littoral states, freedom of navigation and the safety of sea lanes.

This article was originally published in The Hindu *on 10 August 2021, under the headline 'Saudi Arabia, Iran and the possibilities of détente'.*

Chapter 23

Iran's Regional Centrality and Isolation

An essay in *Foreign Affairs* argues that 'Tehran has not achieved any of its lofty ambitions, but it has made progress towards them—and it is feeling emboldened by its recent successes.'[120] It argues that 'Iran is both self-assured and deeply insecure,' 'displays external vigour that conceals ultimately incurable internal maladies,' has 'built its foreign policy on the twin pillars of confronting the United States and Israel,' and is 'closer to realizing its vision than it was a decade ago.' Yet, despite its success in cultivating militant groups across West Asia, there are tangible signs that it has overreached and that two-thirds of young Arabs in the region now view Iran as an adversary. The essay concedes that 'Washington's perception of Iran has suffered from four decades of estrangement and strategic narcissism.' Given the geopolitical and historical backdrop of Iran, does this reflect the totality of the country's interests and strategic perceptions?

A decade earlier, John Limbert, former senior diplomat who was one of the hostages during the embassy siege of 1979, felt that certain rules seemed to guide US policy over the years. These include: (i) never walk through an open door; instead, bang your head against a wall; (ii) never say yes to anything that the other side proposes; doing so will make you weak; and (iii) the other

[120]Sadjadpour, Karim, 'Iran's Hollow Victory,' *Foreign Affairs*, 16 February 2022, https://tinyurl.com/ye8r4h8h. Accessed on 22 November 2025.

side is infinitely hostile, devious, domineering and irrational. It is the embodiment of all that is evil.

POLITICAL STABILITY

With an area of 1.6 million sq. km, Iran is the 18th largest country in the world in terms of area. It shares land borders with Pakistan, Afghanistan, Turkmenistan, Azerbaijan, Armenia, Turkey and Iraq, and maritime borders with Kuwait, Bahrain, Saudi Arabia, Qatar, the UAE and Oman. In its long history, it has experienced periods of conflict, imperial dominance and foreign occupation, and most recently, a revolution. All these left a mark on its collective memory. Its culture has been hugely influential in world history and rightly depicted as an 'Empire of the Mind'.

Since the revolution of 1979, and the end of the US security umbrella under the latter's Twin Pillars policy, Iran has been concerned about national security given its long and porous borders with Iraq and Afghanistan. Refugees have poured in from Afghanistan and an armed aggression resulted in the decade-long war with Iraq. With Pakistan, there was a moment of unease after the Bangladesh War of 1971, but it was soon set at rest by India.

Despite the upheavals of the post-revolutionary era and the war, Iran maintained a degree of political stability. This was thanks to its power structure, based on a multitude of loosely connected and fiercely competitive power centres. These power centres remain formally grounded in the Constitution and its structure as well as in the religio-political characteristics of the clerical leadership that retains an exclusive grip on state power. Each power centre is also embroiled in factional tussles over the facilitation or obstruction of state policies. The locus of individual decisions therefore is always a challenging exercise.

Revolutionary slogans apart, Iran's foreign policy has focused on safeguarding independence, national sovereignty and national interests, and is characterized by conscious adjustment to the reality of regional interests in what has been described as the reality of strategic loneliness. This was evident in the ambivalent reaction to the US attack on Iraq.

The end of the Khomeini era, and the period of Hashemi Rafsanjani, witnessed Iran's attempts to regain a role in regional affairs. These initiatives were built upon by the former president Mohammad Khatami. A beginning was made with regional policy envisaging three circles: the Persian Gulf, the Arab East and Eurasia.

RELATIONSHIP WITH THE US

Apart from other matters, contention between the West and Iran developed on the latter's nuclear energy plans, which were initially developed before the revolution with US assistance, but viewed very differently, subsequently. Iranian scientists in the meantime developed them to a stage at which alarm bells were sounded about their intention.

All of this is reflected in Iran's relationship with the US, which underwent an overnight transition. Initially an ally, Iran became hostile and bitter in individual and national terms. Over time, the perception tended to change; in the past three decades, attempts have been made to mend matters. There were many issues of contention, each with its own subjective angles, but they came to be focused on the nuclear question.

In May 2003, and after America's success in the Iraq war, Iran offered full negotiations with the US through a Swiss intermediary. This was ignored by the George Bush administration. In October 2003, the Tehran Declaration was reached between Iran and the European Union (EU). Iran agreed to cooperate fully with the International Atomic Energy Agency (IAEA) including the Additional Protocol, and agreed to temporarily suspend uranium enrichment. In September and October 2003, the IAEA conducted several facility inspections. In July 2015, the Joint Comprehensive Plan of Action (JCPOA) was concluded between Iran and the P5+1 and the EU. The Donald Trump administration certified Iran's compliance with the agreements twice in 2017, but in May 2018, withdrew from it promising a better deal. This did not happen.

After changes of administration in both Tehran and Washington, quiet negotiations were resumed in Vienna in the expectation of an early success with Iranian insistence on returning to the original terms of the JCPOA. The Ukraine War and the Western regime of sanctions on Russia became an impediment; so did the Iranian insistence that US sanctions be lifted on the Islamic Revolutionary Guard Corps, so effective in Iraq, Syria and with Hezbollah, and also playing a role in the Iranian economy. Some of the Gulf Cooperation Council states are supporting a powerful pro-US lobby in this endeavour.

Despite being a victim of the regime of sanctions for long, Iran has been unrelenting in the development of military technologies. This is evident from its growing capabilities for asymmetric warfare in the region and its success in creating conventionally armed, precision-guided missiles and more effective air defence. Alongside, the apprehension of Iran crossing the much-dreaded nuclear threshold in a region that has India, Pakistan and Israel (undeclared) as nuclear-capable nations is also present. Some experts believe that if the stalemate in negotiations continues, Iran may even give notice of withdrawal from the Non-Proliferation Treaty and, in a play on Israel's policy of 'strategic ambiguity', opt for an approach of 'creative ambiguity'.

In the final analysis, the US has a difficult choice between its strategic objectives, requirements and capabilities in West Asia in relation to Israel and the conservative Arab bloc on the one hand, and with the reality of Iran's regional centrality and its implications, on the other. The failure of the so-called Arab Spring and the formalization of the Abraham Accords is one aspect of it. Its domestic political compulsions and those of Israel were well reflected by the Israeli scholar Martin Kramer in 2011: 'In Israel we are for the status quo. Not only do we believe the status quo is sustainable, we think it is the job of the US to sustain it.'[121] To overcome this impasse, the centrality of Iran in its own neighbourhood has to be recognized along with the latter's commitment to regional cooperation.

This article was originally published in The Hindu *on 23 May 2022, under the headline 'Iran's centrality and isolation'.*

[121]Parsi, Trita, 'Arab Spring Seen from Tehran', The *Cairo Review of Global Affairs*, https://tinyurl.com/4vvsbxcj. Accessed on 24 November 2025.

Chapter 24

The Key in Persian Gulf Littoral

The United Nations defines the body of water between Iran and the Arabian Peninsula as the Persian Gulf. The lands around it are shared by eight countries (Bahrain, Iran, Iraq, Kuwait, Oman, Qatar, Saudi Arabia, and the United Arab Emirates), all members of the UN. There is a commonality of interest among them in being major producers of crude oil and natural gas, and thereby contributing critically to the global economy and to their own prosperity. This has added to their geopolitical significance. At the same time, turbulence has often characterized their inter se political relations.

A FRAMEWORK

For eight decades prior to 1970, this body of water was a closely guarded British lake, administered in good measure by imperial civil servants from India. When that era ended, regional players sought to assert themselves. Imperatives of rivalry and cooperation became evident and, as a United States State Department report put it in 1973, 'The upshot of all these cross-currents is that the logic of Saudi-Iranian cooperation is being undercut by psychological, nationalistic, and prestige factors, which are likely to persist for a long time.'[122] The Nixon and the Carter Doctrines

[122]Ansari, Hamid, 'In Persian Gulf littoral, Cooperative Security is Key', *The Hindu*, 8 June 2020, https://tinyurl.com/svhtt9w9. Accessed on 22 November 2025

were the logical outcome to ensure American hegemony. An early effort for collective security, attempted in a conference in Muscat in 1975, was thwarted by Baathist Iraq. The Iranian Revolution put an end to the Twin Pillar approach and disturbed the strategic balance. The Iraq-Iran War enhanced US interests and role. Many moons and much bloodshed later, it was left to the Security Council through Resolution 598 (1987) to explore 'measures to enhance the security and stability in the region'[123].

Any framework for stability and security thus needs to answer a set of questions: security for whom, by whom, against whom, for what purpose? Is the requirement in local, regional or global terms? Does it require an extra-regional agency? Given the historical context, one recalls a Saudi scholar's remark in the 1990s that 'Gulf regional security was an external issue long before it was an issue among the Gulf States themselves.'[124]

The essential ingredients of such a framework would thus be to ensure conditions of peace and stability in individual littoral states; freedom to all states of the Gulf littoral to exploit their hydrocarbon and other natural resources and export them; freedom of commercial shipping in international waters of the Persian Gulf; freedom of access to, and outlet from, Gulf waters through the Strait of Hormuz; prevention of conflict that may impinge on the freedom of trade and shipping; and prevention of emergence of conditions that may impinge on any of these considerations. Could such a framework be self-sustaining or require external guarantees for its operational success? If the latter, what should its parameters be?

---

[123]'The Situation between Iran and Iraq', *Security Council Report*, https://tinyurl.com/7hkpv79u. Accessed on 25 November 2025.

[124]Ansari, Hamid, 'In Persian Gulf littoral, Cooperative Security is Key', *The Hindu*, 8 June 2020, https://tinyurl.com/svhtt9w9. Accessed on 22 November 2025.

THE GCC AND THE US LINK

The past two decades have revalidated William Fulbright's observation that statesmen often confuse great power with total power and great responsibility with total responsibility. The war in Iraq and its aftermath testify to it. The US effort to 'contain' the Iranian revolutionary forces, supplemented by the effort of the Arab states of the littoral (except Iraq) through the instrumentality of the Gulf Cooperation Council, or GCC (May 1981), to coordinate, cooperate and integrate to 'serve the sublime objectives of the Arab Nation' initially met with success in some functional fields and a lack of it in its wider objectives.

In the meantime, geopolitical factors and conflicts elsewhere in the West Asian region—Yemen, Syria, Libya—aggravated global and regional relationships and hampered a modus vivendi in US-Iran relations that was to be premised on the multilateral agreement on Iran's nuclear programme agreed to by Western powers and the Obama Administration, but disowned by US President Donald Trump whose strident policies have taken the region to the brink of an armed conflict.

Perceptions of declining US commitment to sub-regional security have been articulated in recent months amid hints of changing priorities. This is reported to have caused disquiet in some, perhaps all, members of the GCC, the hub of whose security concern remains pivoted on an Iranian threat (political and ideological rather than territorial) and an American insurance to deter it based on a convergence of interests in which oil, trade, arms purchases, etc., have a role to play, along with wider US regional and global determinants.

AN EVOLVING TRANSFORMATION

It is evident that a common GCC threat perception has not evolved over time and has been hampered by the emergence of conflicting tactical and strategic interests and subjective considerations. The current divisions within the organization are therefore here to stay. These have been aggravated by the global economic crisis, the immediate and long-term impact of Covid-19 on regional economies, the problems in the Organization of the Petroleum Exporting Countries (OPEC), and the decline in oil prices.

One credible assessment done recently suggests that in the emerging shape of the region, 'Saudi Arabia is a fading power, UAE, Qatar and Iran are emerging as the new regional leaders, and Oman and Iraq will have to struggle to retain their sovereign identities. The GCC is effectively ended, and OPEC is becoming irrelevant as oil policy moves to a tripartite global condominium. None of this will necessarily happen overnight and external intervention could interfere in unexpected ways. [...] But it is fair to say that the Persian Gulf as we have known for at least three generations is in the midst of a fundamental transformation.'

With the Arab League entombed and the GCC on life-support system, the Arab states of this sub-region are left to individual devices to explore working arrangements with Iraq and Iran. The imperatives for these are different but movement on both is discernible. With Iran in particular and notwithstanding the animosities of the past, pragmatic approaches of recent months seem to bear fruit. Oman has always kept its lines of communication with Iran open; Kuwait and Qatar had done likewise but in a quieter vein, and now the UAE has initiated pragmatic arrangements. These could set the stage for a wider dialogue. Both Iran and the GCC states would benefit from a formal commitment to an arrangement incorporating the six points listed above; so would every outside nation that has trading and economic interests in the Gulf. This could be sanctified by a global convention.

Record shows that the alternative of exclusive security arrangements promotes armament drives, enhances insecurity and aggravates regional tensions. It unavoidably opens the door for Great Power interference.

INDIA'S TIES

How does India perceive these developments and how do they impact our strategic interests and concerns? Locating the Persian Gulf littoral with reference to India is an exercise in geography and history. The distance from Mumbai to Basra is 1,526 nautical miles; Bandar Abbas and Dubai are in a radius of slightly over 1,000 nautical miles from Mumbai. The bilateral relationship, economic and political, with the GCC has blossomed in recent years. The governments are India-friendly and Indian-friendly and appreciate the benefits of a wide-ranging relationship. This is well reflected in the bilateral trade of around $121 billion and remittances of $49 billion from a workforce of over nine million. GCC suppliers account for around 34 per cent of our crude imports, and national oil companies in Saudi Arabia and Abu Dhabi are partners in a $44 billion investment in the giant Ratnagiri oil refinery. In addition, Saudi Aramco is reported to take a 20 per cent stake in Reliance oil-to-chemicals business. The current adverse impact of the pandemic on our economic relations with the GCC countries has now become a matter of concern.

The relationship with Iran, complex at all times and more so recently on account of overt American pressure, has economic potential and geopolitical relevance on account of its actual or alleged role in Pakistan and Afghanistan. Iran also neighbours Turkey and some countries of Central Asia, the Caucasus and the Caspian Sea region. Its size, politico-technological potential and economic resources cannot be wished away, regionally and globally, but can be harnessed for wider good.

India has eschewed involvement in local or regional disputes. Indian interests do not entail power projection; they necessitate, in their totality, peace and regional stability, freedom of navigation and access to the region's markets in terms of trade, technology and manpower resources. Indian interests would be best served if this stability is ensured through cooperative security since the alternative—of competitive security options—cannot ensure durable peace.

This article was originally published in The Hindu *on 8 June 2020, under the headline 'In Persian Gulf littoral, cooperative security is key'.*

Chapter 25

We and Our Neighbourhood: Security and Regional Cooperation

The conceptual framework of our discourse for this piece is premised on the meaning and implications of 'neighbourhood'. In its simplest sense, it is a locality or an area, the place of habitation of some people, bounded by physical features and demographic and socioeconomic characteristics.

Geographically speaking, our region and the surrounding and adjourning seas are depicted as South or Southern Asia. It is inhabited by humans who number around 1.8 billion. They are citizens or residents of a number of political entities, are not homogenous, and have multiple identities amongst them and within them. In socioeconomic terms, they are depicted as 'developing countries' and (with the exception of Sri Lanka) figure in the Medium Human Development category of the HD indices of UNDP.

The countries of the region are characterized by disparities of size and population and dissimilarities of economic structures, levels of development and political systems. Together they propel both positive and negative impulses on human, instrumentalist and conceptual dimensions of neighbourhood; these are not frozen and monolithic concepts and have to be probed empirically.

The human impulses are evident enough. It emanates from the relationship of living environment and its social shape emanating from the family unit and developing into larger groups and societies.

The instrumentalist compulsions naturally follow since sheer necessity compels social groups and societies to organize themselves for common good. To do so, they need rules of the game for common good. Thus, justice becomes the first virtue of social institutions.

By the same logic, the idea of neighbourhood implies physical proximity. So social groupings including political entities or states so situated require rules of engagement and develop codes of conduct for seeking common good and avoiding or minimizing conflicts.

Thus, neighbours on the one hand seek security from each other, and on the other, avenues of cooperation for mutual benefit. The two are not exclusive and are used interchangeably in a variety of ways that have been written about down the ages. Similarly, the concept of comprehensive security covers physical, economic and environmental security as well as security of resources.

It is truism that while friends and enemies can be chosen, neighbours are a gift or a curse of the Maker or of human folly; neither can be undone easily and therefore have to be lived with.

It is evident that possible patterns of interaction between neighbours cover the entire range of human relationships. These range from situations of conflict to those of peaceful coexistence and active cooperation.

Historically, the best-known cases of interaction relate to wars or warlike situations. These could be conventional or non-conventional and continue to be studied for insights.

Change is a rule of life and adaptability a necessity. Some may have come across Prof. Sean McFate's recently published work on *The New Rules of War* and his contention that the future would be a period of 'Durable Disorder' in which the world will not collapse into anarchy but rule-based order will crumble to be replaced by armed conflicts fought mostly by covert means. In it, plausible deniability will be more effective than firepower, traditional battles will not prove decisive, and victory will be won or lost in the information space, not on the physical battlefield. His effort to update Sun Tzu's maxims makes for interesting reading.

WAKE-UP CALLS

Be that as it may, my purpose is to share some thoughts on a more relevant aspect of security. I refer to human security, meaning comprehensive, prevention-oriented security of people, defined in a UN resolution as 'survival, livelihood and dignity' for those who inhabit the states for whom we seek security in military terms. Thus, military security becomes one—albeit very important—aspect of the overall comprehensive human security that we seek individually and collectively.

What then are the dimensions of human security in South Asia and its implications for regional cooperation in our neighbourhood?

The UNDP's Human Development Report for 2018 notes that based on our environmental indicators, 'today's progress is coming at the expense of our children.' A changing climate, massive declines in biodiversity, and the depletion of land and freshwater resources pose serious threats to humankind. They require an immediate and ambitious change in production and consumption patterns since environmental degradation puts human development gains at risk, and coupled with significant declines in biodiversity, it is linked to other development concerns ranging from declining food and water supplies to losses of livelihood and life from extreme weather events.

This profoundly serious crisis, according to the Report, threatens the human development of current and future generations. It asserts that business-as-usual approaches must change, with countries at different levels of human development exposed to and contributing to environmental degradation in different ways.

Linked to climate change and biodiversity loss, deforestation also degrades land and reduces the quantity and quality of freshwater. The overall pace of forest loss has slowed in recent years, but the planet still lost 3.2 per cent of its forests between 1990 and 2015. Low-human-development countries, many of them reservoirs of global biodiversity, lost 14.5 per cent.

Freshwater withdrawals stand at 7.2 per cent of the global supply, with vast differences across countries and regions. In South Asia, annual withdrawals stand at 23.8 per cent of total renewable supplies. Unsustainable water withdrawals and inadequate treatment of waste contaminate drinking water, with cascading impacts on health, employment and gender inequality. While every ingredient of the emerging scenario has disturbing implications, perhaps the latter, water, is the most critical and has relevance for our discussion today.

A scholar who wrote a tome some years back on the geopolitics of water in Asia analysed the problems along four dimensions: water shortage, water stress, water scarcity and water insecurity. Citing a UN report, he concluded that 'Asia seems to live beyond its means.' The reason for this he attributed partly to lesser fresh water per capita available compared to other regions of the globe and partly to unsustainable practices that have upset hydrological cycles.

In an Asia-wide perspective, the study brought out 'the unique triple role of Tibet as Asia's water repository, water supplier and rainmaker, and thereby underscores the centrality of the Tibetan Plateau on the Asian water map.'

What is true of the Asian continent as a whole is particularly true of South Asia both on account of its large population—1.9 billion in 2019, expected to go up to 2.1 billion in 2030—and its much greater percentage of cultivated land under irrigation. The same holds for the exploitation of groundwater resources. Two of the largest countries of the region, India and Pakistan, are already in the *water stress* category.

One visible consequence of this is the presence of both intrastate and interstate conflicts relating to water. Most of us are familiar with some aspects of river water disputes within our own country, disputes that have defied solutions for decades.

The irony is that compared to these, the resolution of interstate river water disputes have had a much better success record. I refer to the Indus Water Treaty between India and Pakistan, the Ganges Treaty between India and Bangladesh, and the Mahakali Treaty between India and Nepal. None of these could have been possible without bilateral cooperation balancing mutual gains and concessions. They are premised on volumetric allocation of river flows, contain but do not eliminate tensions, and stop short of basin-wide river management regime.

A long-term holistic approach has been suggested but remains to be implemented. It requires regional cooperation in greater measure since the present arrangement is unlikely to be sustained in perpetuity given the rising populations and the pressures on land and water resources. It is thus inevitable that renewable resources will be depleted and the prospects of new battle lines over trans-boundary water resources may not be far-fetched and requires imaginative thinking about the future. Thus, four questions need to be addressed:

- Can water resources be enhanced?
- Can water usage be rationalized?
- Can domestic policies on water utilization and depletion of trans-border aquifers be coordinated in the region?
- Can wider water cooperation that would include river basins beyond South Asia be visualized?

The conclusion I draw from this is that there is an imperative need for seeking security through regional cooperation on water resources in our neighbourhood. Given the inter-linkages with other environment-related matters, this cooperation cannot be confined to water only and has to extend to all related matters affecting environmental security. None of this, however, can materialize unless there is a realization of the urgency of the matter.

How is this to be initiated? As in the case of conventional security and warfare in this new age, the traditional approach to human security—of proceeding principally through political coordination—may not suffice and the experience of recent decades does not encourage it. The obvious example is SAARC wherein disagreements between two important members have resulted in an impasse and the virtual abandonment of the political leadership of this organization. Yet, almost the entire region is an integrated environmental unit in which the environmental and ecological issues are interlinked and cannot be addressed piecemeal. They also transcend political borders.

Some observers, basing themselves on the reported retreat of Himalayan glaciers and the deforestation that has taken place, have opined that 'it is a disaster waiting to happen'. In one projection, with a 2°C rise in global temperature, net cereal production in South Asian countries is projected to decline by 4 to 10 per cent by the end of this century. We should also see this in the context of global warming for which sufficient evidence is now available the world over.

Here there is scope for looking at the experience of other regions. A good example is what we now know as the European Union. Given the long history of wars between France and Germany, the then French foreign minister Robert Schuman proposed in 1950 'a way to make war not only unthinkable but materially impossible' by creating a community of interests in the shape of the European Coal and Steel Community to help the economy of Europe rebuild itself. An American impulse in the shape of the Marshal Plan assisted the process. Over time it developed into the EEC and then into the EU. Its current mechanisms for economic, defence and political cooperation include the issue of climate change.

Thus, political cooperation can move in tandem with a basic understanding on matters that are of mutual benefit.

The question to be addressed is this: if a commonality of interests can be identified beginning with economic interest, and result in benefits to all concerned, why can it not be developed on matters of human survival relating to water, environment and ecology? The scholar cited above had suggested some approaches of preventive diplomacy to forestall water wars by building cooperative institutional mechanism like Asian norms and rules that cover trans-border water resources and manage water competition. Little progress however has been made in implementing them.

I am realistic enough to admit that such an exercise in futurology relating to human survival goes beyond the responsibilities of soldiers and diplomats and rests squarely with those entrusted with the destiny of nations. Yet, both soldiers and diplomats can contribute to the effort by delineating what Alan Kay, a scientist in a computer research laboratory, said in 1971: 'The best way to predict the future is to invent it.'

Can I be bold enough to imagine that we in India, with our civilization's heritage of cosmic insight, will contribute to this venture?

This was originally a talk delivered to course trainees at the National Defence College on the subject 'We and Our Neighbourhood: Security and Regional Cooperation', on 31 July 2019.

Chapter 26

India and the Persian Gulf at the Dawn of the 21st Century

Locating the Persian Gulf in relation to India is an exercise in geography and history. The distance from Mumbai to Basra is 1,526 nautical miles and Basra, strictly speaking, is beyond the Gulf. Bandar Abbas and Dubai are within a radius of 1,000 nautical miles. Widely used words, expressions and proverbs in the region are reflective of the depth of the Gulf's relations with India.[125]

From the earliest times the sea was, and remains, the link. All parts of the Persian Gulf traded with the west coast of India. Very often, the Gulf served as a transit route for trading destinations in the further reaches of western and central Asia. The commodity mix of this trade, and of the relationships that accompanied it, changed with the requirements of the day. Above all and at all times, the links were primarily of people. Evidence of this is to be found in the colloquial language of the two regions and even more so in proverbs. The travelogue of the 10th-century shipmaster Buzurg Ibn Shahriyar, *The Book of the Wonders of India*, makes

---

[125]The uses of the proper noun 'Hind', and its derivatives, establish the affinity and admiration that early residents of the Arabian Peninsula had for India. The Arabic word for engineering (*hindesa*) and for swords made of Indian steel (*muhannad*) testify to areas of excellence in mathematics and technology. The historian Tabari reports an equally telling legend: 'The land with the sweetest smell on earth is the land of India.' *The History of Al-Tabari, Volume I*, State University of New York Press, New York, 1989, p. 291.

evident the Gulf's fascination with India.

The 19th-century traveller Burckhardt gave an accurate description of the Indian business presence in Makkah:

> Trade is carried out by means of brokers, many of whom are Indians: in general, the community of Indians is the wealthiest in Mecca. They are in direct communication with all the harbors of Hindustan and they can often afford to undersell their competitors. Many of them [...] are stationary here, while others are constantly travelling backward and forward between India and Hijaz. They retain their native language, which they teach to their children, and also many merchants of Mecca superficially, so that most of the latter understand, at least the Hindustani numerals and the most ordinary phrases in buying and selling [...] They are shrewd traders, and an overmatch, sometimes, even for the Arabians.

Since the advent of European rule in Asia, control of the Gulf in strategic terms was considered essential for the defence of colonial possessions in India. The British doctrine of supremacy was formally proclaimed by the Viceroy of India at Sharjah in November 1903: 'The peace of these waters must be maintained: your independence will continue to be upheld, and the influence of the British government must remain supreme.'[126] This was reiterated in 1928 in London by the Committee on Imperial Defence: 'No foreign power must be allowed to establish a naval base or a fortified fort in the Gulf or air undertakings within striking distance of it.'[127]

In recent times, the Persian Gulf region has been an area of

---

[126]Lorimer, J.G., *Gazetteer of the Persian Gulf, Oman and Central Arabia, Volume I Part II*, Calcutta, 1915, p. 39.

[127]Abdullah, Mohammad Morsy, *The United Arab Emirates*, Routledge, London, 1978, p. 43.

turbulence, contributed in no small measure by external factors. This period has coincided with an enormous enhancement in the economic and strategic relevance of the Gulf. In the foreseeable future, its oil and gas resources will be critical to meeting the world's growing appetite for energy. According to the International Energy Agency, 'its share of world oil production would jump from 35% in 2004 to 44% in 2030.'

The Persian Gulf is thus a familiar region for independent India. It is also an area of opportunity for an India that is beginning to register its presence in economic and strategic terms. It could also be a source of dislocations, even problems. A closer monitoring of the developments in the region, and of the interplay of global forces at work there, is thus of relevance to India's strategic planning.

Paradoxically, the familiarity of Indians with the region has resulted in the 'Gulf factor' taking a backseat in India's strategic perceptions. The region sits astride the north-western approaches to India, accounts for 70 per cent of imported energy supplies, is the destination for an expanding export basket that has traditional as well as new items and services, and plays host to an Indian workforce of 3.5 million who repatriate about $7 billion annually. In monetary terms, the India-Persian Gulf relationship is worth around US$18 billion. Geopolitical considerations add to this in considerable measure.

I

In recent times, the late 1960s constitute a valid point of reference for assessing the national security perceptions of the concerned regional states, and of India.

In November 1970, the US National Security Council pronounced that the United States had only 'minimal security interests in the Persian Gulf'. In January 1980, the Carter Doctrine proclaimed to the contrary and said that 'any attempt by an outside force to gain control of the Persian Gulf region will be regarded as an assault on the vital interests of the United States.'[128]

A beginning could be made with Iran. In the mid-sixties, the Iranian monarchy had overcome (with the CIA's overt assistance) the trauma of the Mossadeq years and driven underground the clerical opposition. Relieved of these domestic worries, the Shah felt confident enough to assert the claim of Iran to the leadership of the Gulf, grounded in the physical reality of (a) having a 1,200-km coastline on the Gulf, (b) being with Oman the joint controller of the strategic tanker routes in the Straits of Hormuz, (c) having through the Gulf its own lifeline for oil exports, (d) being the only non-Arab state in the Persian Gulf littoral, (e) being a frontline ally of the West in the Cold War, and (f) having friendly ties with Israel and, after the Six-Day War of June 1967, no longer being threatened by Arab nationalism. Even earlier in 1962, the Shah had signalled a change of policy towards the Soviet Union by refusing to accept US missile bases on Iranian soil and, after the Indo-Pak conflict of 1965, had come to the conclusion that CENTO's protective cover 'did not mean a commitment to defend Iran in terms of his local threats as he saw them.' He had therefore decided to build up Iran's own defence capability. In a statement in March 1965, he announced that his military preparations would henceforth be focused on the Persian Gulf. Substance to it was added in the Turkey-Iran-Pakistan communiqué of December 1967 wherein it was asserted that the responsibility for the preservation of peace and stability in the Persian Gulf rested only with the littoral states.[129] These perceptions of Iran were reinforced in the period after the British

---

[128]Palmer, Michael A., *Guardians of the Gulf: A History of America's Expanding Role in the Persian Gulf*, Touchstone, New York, 1992, pp. 85–111.

[129]Cottrell, Alvin J., 'Iran and the Persian Gulf: Political, Military, and Economic Considerations', Testimony before the US House of Representatives Subcommittee on the Near East and South Asia, 24 July 1973.

withdrawal and in the context of the 'Twin Pillar' approach of the United States to security in the Gulf.

At the other end of the spectrum was Iraq. The Revolution of 1958 made Iraq the only non-monarchical state in the Gulf littoral. Iraq's espousal of Arab nationalism and its denunciation of the Western alliance system made her a formidable frontline adversary of Iran and compounded the longstanding disagreements between the two neighbours relating to the land borders and the Shatt-al-Arab question, and the Treaty of 1937. In March 1967, according to the former Iranian Ambassador Jaafar Raed, President Abdul Rahman Arif and the Shah agreed that the Shatt-al-Arab dispute would be resolved to Iran's satisfaction in return for Iran settling other disputes with Iraq and stopping its support to the Kurds. A joint communiqué issued after this meeting spoke of the water of the boundary rivers being used according to international law.[130] There was however some delay in the implementing of this understanding; the Arab-Israeli War of June 1967 may have influenced perceptions. Arif, in any case, was overthrown in the Baath coup of July 1968 and policies of the new Iraqi government aggravated matters further. In April 1969, Iran unilaterally abrogated the 1937 treaty. Regional developments and Cold War alignments hardened positions. In this context, Iraq's denunciation of Iran's occupation of the Gulf islands was in step with known policy perceptions. Henry Kissinger has recorded for posterity a conversation with Zhou Enlai in April 1973 in which the Chinese premier stressed that 'the United States needed to take great care to prevent radical Iraq from achieving hegemony in the Persian Gulf,' adding that 'the Shah of Iran, in contrast, was a far-sighted leader who understood the world.'[131] Kissinger also reported the Shah's remark that he 'would keep Iraq occupied by supporting the

[130]Souresrafil, Behrouz, *The Iran-Iraq War*, Plainview, New York, 1989, p. 14.

[131]Kissinger, Henry, *Years of Upheaval*, Little Brown, Boston, 1982, p. 687.

Kurdish rebellion within Iraq and maintaining a large army near the frontier.'[132] The rationale for this approach was the perceived threat from a radical Iraq to the moderate pro-Western regimes in the area, as also the fear of Soviet inroads typified in the Iraq-USSR Friendship Treaty of April 1972. (Despite the commitments in the Treaty, however, Moscow consciously kept a balance in relations with Iran, did not endorse Iraq's position on the Gulf islands, and, in October 1972, it concluded with Iran a 15-year treaty of economic and technical cooperation.)[133] The resulting tensions in Iran-Iraq relations persisted for several years but were also accompanied by quiet attempts to resolve problems. In January 1975, the Iranian foreign minister, in a meeting with his Iraqi counterpart in Istanbul, reverted to the 1967 understanding and suggested that if Iraq accepted Iran's objectives in the Shatt-al-Arab, then Iran would also show flexibility on the question of the land borders. These ideas were eventually incorporated in the Algiers Accord of March 1975 and in the two treaties signed in June 1975, proclaiming a 'final and permanent solution to all problems pending between the two countries.'

The third major player amongst the littoral states is Saudi Arabia. Its traditional concern has been with its land borders and with its drive for primacy in the Arabian Peninsula. In the 1964-67 period, the Saudis were preoccupied with the threat of Arab radicalism on their border with Yemen. Egypt's defeat in the Six-Day War resolved that problem but another one surfaced

[132]Ibid., 675.

[133]Shemesh, Haim, *Soviet-Iraqi Relations, 1968-1988: In the Shadow of the Iraq-Iran Conflict*, Lynne Rienner Publishers, Boulder, Colorado, 1992, p. 85. The Soviet-Iranian joint communique of October 1972 also asserted that 'questions relating to the Persian Gulf area should be settled in accordance with the principles of the UN Charter by states of the area themselves without any interference from outside.' (See Shubin, S., and S. Zabih, *The Foreign Relations of Iran*, University of California Press, 1974, p. 265.)

with the British withdrawal from Aden and its replacement by the PDRY, a regime with a Marxist orientation. The Saudi effort to use the YAR to counter the PDRY met with only limited success, and South Yemen's support to the Dhofar rebellion—and the involvement in the latter of the world's communist powers—compelled the Saudis to normalize relations with Oman and endorse Iran's military involvement, on the side of the Sultan of Oman, in the Dhofar fighting. These wider strategic considerations prompted Saudi Arabia to seek and obtain the support of the Shah of Iran for their Islamic conference initiative and, as a quid pro quo, they allowed the Shah—after he had agreed to Bahrain's independence—to project his role in the security of the Gulf after the departure of the British.

This cosy arrangement was upset by the oil crisis of 1973 and the inflow of the new oil wealth to the oil exporting countries. A new Iranian assertiveness in the Gulf was one result of it; another was the moderation of Iraqi postures, and a search for accommodation with the United States and with the conservative Arab regimes. In the 1973–75 period therefore, Saudi policy counted on the US to check Iran and on Iran to check Iraq, and thus maintain a balance deemed desirable by Riyadh. In the period after the Algiers Accord, however, Saudi endeavour was to use Iraq to slow down or neutralize the Shah's scheme of a regional collective security pact—which would necessarily result in an Iranian domination—and simultaneously use Iran to oppose Iraq's move for a series of bilateral pacts between Iraq and the Arab states of the Gulf—which in turn would ensure a pivotal position for Iraq. On Iranian insistence on pursuing the matter further, in April 1975 Saudi Arabia spelt out for the first time its own ideas in a set of five principles: (a) exclusion of the superpowers from the Gulf; (b) denial of military bases to any of the superpowers; (c) military cooperation among the Gulf countries to ensure freedom of navigation through the Straits of

Hormuz; (d) peaceful resolution of regional disputes; and (e) a collective guarantee for the territorial integrity of all the states of the Gulf.[134] This, in the Shah's view, fell short of his notion of collective security; Iraq, on the other hand, still saw an Iranian hegemony in any such development.

At that stage Oman, perhaps on Iranian prompting, called a meeting of the foreign ministers of the littoral states in Muscat on 25–26 November 1975.[135] Discussion centred on six items: (1) limitation on the presence of foreign powers in the region; (2) a guarantee of the territorial integrity of states; (3) a non-aggression pact; (4) mutual assistance against subversion and cooperation in intelligence; (5) measures to ensure freedom of navigation; and (6) a territorial division of Gulf waters and establishment of the limits of the continental shelf. A number of papers submitted by the participants were discussed but no conclusions were arrived at. Difficulties arose on account of an Iranian proposal to have a unified, multilateral military force under a joint command to deal with both internal and external defence needs, and also to have a more restrictive legal regime for innocent passage through the Straits of Hormuz. Both suggestions were opposed by Iraq. Saudi Arabia refused to be drawn into these differences and Kuwait's attempt at mediation failed.

A month before this meeting, the Saudis had proposed a pact on internal security amongst the Arab states of the Gulf; this too had failed to elicit adequate support. Finally, in June 1978, in the wake of developments in the Horn of Africa, apprehensions about the security of the oil route resurfaced, and the Shah revived the

---

[134]Safran, Nadav, *Saudi Arabia: The Ceaseless Quest for Security*, Harvard University Press, 1985, p. 267. Also, Holden, David, and Richard Johns, *The House of Saud*, Macmillan, London, 1981, p. 425.

[135]Chubin, Shahram, *Security in the Persian Gulf, Vol. 4: The Role of Outside Powers*, The International Institute for Strategic Studies, U.K., 1982, pp. 152–153.

idea of joint defence arrangements.[136] The April 1978 Taraki coup in Afghanistan seemed to have some impact on Iraqi perceptions, and a new proposal circulated by Oman in May 1978 brought forth a positive response from Baghdad. As a result, negotiations took place in June between Iraq, Iran and Saudi Arabia but suspicions of Iran again came in the way. Yet another effort to bridge the gap was made by Crown Prince Fahd when he visited Baghdad in August. By then, however, the internal developments in Iran and the pressure of these on the Shah had given rise to another set of concerns in Baghdad and Riyadh.

The extent of the ground covered in this period in the Iranian-Saudi quest to develop a common perception on regional and regime security questions was revealed in 1993 by a Saudi author privy to the views of his government. The two countries, according to him, reached 'broad agreement on a number of principles: (1) the need to keep the Gulf region out of the superpowers` armed conflicts; (2) the need to ensure that foreign military bases were not established in the Gulf region; (3) the need for the Gulf states to build their own military power in order to defend themselves; (4) the need for a collective security arrangement in the Gulf region; (5) the need for all Gulf countries to maintain a reliable internal security force that could enforce law and order and deal effectively with any domestic threat; (6) the need to combat all kinds of terrorism by all possible means; and (7) the need to stand against all radical and extremist groups and movements that aim at disturbing the security and stability in the region in particular and the Middle East in general.'[137] Both countries also developed a limited measure of intelligence cooperation through the 'Safari Club' whose other members were France, Egypt and Morocco.[138]

[136]Safran, N., op. cit., pp. 272–275.

[137]Badeeb, Saeed M., *Saudi-Iranian Relations 1932-1982*, Echoes, London, 1993, p. 125.

[138]Ibid., 130–131.

The Iranian Revolution (February 1979) brought into being a wholly new situation: 'It disturbed the strategic balance in the region,'[139] and put an end to the post-1975 efforts to develop a regional consensus on security issues. The siege of the Grand Mosque in Makkah in November 1979 and the induction of the Soviet army in Afghanistan in December generated a new threat perception and propelled the principal actors to opt for other means to safeguard their interests. The Carter doctrine was the inevitable outcome of the situation.

An observer surveying the scene in early 1980 would thus have noted that perceptions hitherto bore the clear imprint of the preceding century and rested solely on the possible options to replace the British 'command of the sea' doctrine. For convenience of analysis, these could be categorized into five groups: (a) one country, i.e. Iran, staking its claim to act as the policeman of the Gulf; (b) the Twin Pillar policy of entrusting responsibility to Iran and Saudi Arabia; (c) the major Gulf-powers approach focused on Iran, Iraq and Saudi Arabia; (d) a web of bilateral security arrangements on the Arab side of the Gulf; and (e) a comprehensive pact entered into by all the littoral states. With regard to contents, proposals ranged from (1) freedom of navigation in the Straits of Hormuz to (2) the placement of a mechanism for the peaceful settlement of disputes and a collective guarantee for the territorial integrity of the member states, and (3) the exclusion of foreign powers and foreign bases. Developments throughout the 1980–90 period were to show that in order to ensure the first, the goal of the third had to be reversed, and the second relegated to secondary priority!

Whatever else it may or may not have achieved, the Iran-Iraq war did put to test the principle of the freedom of navigation

---

[139]Bakash, Shaul, *The Reign of the Ayatollahs: Iran and the Islamic Revolution*, Basic Books, New York, 1984, p. 4.

through the Straits of Hormuz. The passage was kept open as much by the US armada as by the compulsions of self-interest of all parties. This was spelt out with brutal candour by Rafsanjani in October 1983: 'We will block the Straits of Hormuz when we cannot export oil,' adding carefully that 'even if they (the Iraqis) hit half of our oil, it will not be in our interest to block the Straits of Hormuz.' The bottom line was amplified somewhat in May 1984: 'We would close the Straits of Hormuz if the Persian Gulf becomes unusable for us. And if the Persian Gulf becomes unusable for us, we will make the Persian Gulf unusable for others.'[140]

In terms of the traditional paradigm of security, the two wars in the Gulf (1980–88 and 1990–91) demonstrated in ample measure the potential for instability in the region. In the same period the two attempts made to address the problem, i.e. the formation of the GCC in 1981 and the Damascus Declaration group in 1991, produced inadequate results. The reasons for their failure are to be explored in the nature of these groupings, in the manner in which they sought to achieve their objectives, and in the definition of the objectives themselves.[141]

It has been aptly remarked that Gulf security 'was an external issue long before it was one among the Gulf States themselves.'[142] The foregoing survey of the twenty-year period (1971–91)

---

[140]Ramazani, R.K., *Revolutionary Iran: Challenge and Response in the Middle East*, John Hopkins University Press, 1986, pp. 15–16.

[141]Magnus, Ralph H., 'The G.C.C. and Security: The Enemy Without and the Enemy Within', *The Journal of South Asia and Middle Eastern Studies*, Vol. 20, No. 3, 1997, pp. 72–94.

A detailed analysis of the Damascus Declaration and its aftermath is to be found in Hollis, Rosemary, 'Whatever Happened to the Damascus Declaration: Evolving Security Structures in the Gulf', *Politics and International Relations in the Middle East,* M. Jane Davis (ed.), Edward Elger, Aldershot, U.K. 1995, pp. 37–60; and Wilson, Peter W., and Douglas F. Graham, *Saudi Arabia: The Coming Storm*, M. E. Sharpe, New York, 1994, pp. 131–132 and pp. 164–165.

[142]Badeeb, Saeed M., op. cit., p. 123.

demonstrates the validity of this perception. The reasons are evident: the region around the Gulf is the source of energy; this energy is crucial to the well-being of the industrialized world which requires its uninterrupted flow from the producers to the consumers; since this movement of energy is principally by sea, open sea lanes in the relevant region become a prerequisite; hence the doctrine of the 'command of the sea' which in the post-1971 period transmuted itself into 'control in friendly hands'. This perception was externally induced and in the first instance served the interests of the external powers; however, it failed to enhance regional stability and security. The same was the case with the post-1991 arrangement riveted on the one side to bilateral defence arrangements with external powers, and on the other, to the policy of 'Dual Containment'.

The Iranian Revolution 'helped produce a higher level of political integration between the states of the Arab Gulf'.[143] One result of this political integration was the creation of a token, brigade-sized, rapid deployment force based in Saudi Arabia and composed of troops drawn from all the GCC states. This was found to be totally inadequate at the time of the Kuwait crisis of 1990[144]; the suggestion by Oman, in 1991, to expand it into a force of 100,000 met with no success. One responsible commentator in a GCC country gave his reasons for this: 'In my personal view, the answer (to the need to rethink collective defense arrangements) cannot lie in a force like Peninsula Shield, shaped as much by

---

[143]Suwaidi, Jamal S., 'The Gulf Security Dilemma: The Arab Gulf States, The United States, and Iran', *Iran and the Gulf*, Jamal S. Suwaidi (ed.), Abu Dhabi, 1996, p. 339.

[144]Sultan, HRH General Khalid Bin, *Desert Warrior: A Personal View of the Gulf War by the Joint Forces Commander*, Harper Collins, New Delhi, 1997, pp. 248–249. Also, Al-Mazidi Feisal, *The Future of the Gulf*, I.B. Tauris, London, 1993, pp. 70 –71.

political as by military considerations.'[145] Another felt 'collective security is largely off the agenda, given the current attitude of most GCC governments and their reluctance to lose autonomy over defence and military decision.'[146]

Apart from these political considerations and as Anthony Cordesman has observed, there are differing threat perceptions within the GCC itself:

> It may be tempting for many in the West to divide the Gulf into three parts: Iran, Iraq, and the Southern Gulf and then describe the Southern Gulf in terms of strategic shorthand—using the Gulf Cooperation Council (GCC) as a synonym for all the Southern Gulf states. Any net assessment of the Gulf, however, must focus on the fact that the differences between the Southern Gulf states are as important as are the similarities...Each of the individual Southern Gulf states has different strategic needs and vulnerabilities...As a result, the strategic priorities and military balance in the upper Gulf will always be determined by different factors from those that affect the central and lower Gulf.[147]

The connotation of the term 'security' itself, in national, regional, or global terms, has undergone considerable evolution. In 1943, Walter Lippman defined it in terms of protecting the core values of a country. Two decades later, Arnold Wolfers viewed it as 'the ability of a nation to deter an attack or defeat it'. The Palme Commission (1982) considered it to imply 'both physical and psychological security which may be subject to threats from both internal and external sources.' More recently, it has been described as the 'capacity of a state to deter or counter threats to its three

[145]Sultan, Khalid Bin, op. cit., p. 475.

[146]Al-Mazidi, Feisal, op. cit., p. 72.

[147]Cordesman, Anthony H., *Bahrain, Oman, Qatar, and the UAE: Challenges of Security*, Routledge, Boulder, 1997.

components: territory, society, and regime.'[148] The concept of the security of resources, and of environmental and demographic factors, has also been included to develop a more comprehensive approach. Each of these is relevant to the Persian Gulf littoral.

A new approach was clearly called for. The challenge would seem to lie in developing a (minimum) common threat perception, in maintaining it over time, and in developing the mechanism for minimizing risks to common security and in maximizing the benefits of cooperation. Such a concept of Common or Cooperative Security was enunciated by the Palme Commission; it urged nations of the world to 'replace the doctrine of mutual deterrence' by the idea of common security, go beyond security based on armament which cannot be sustained indefinitely, and instead, seek to create 'positive processes that can lead to peace and disarmament' based on a set of common principles, which were enunciated in some detail, but the application of which in practical terms 'must be tailored to the realities of political and military circumstances in specific situations.'[149] Others have contributed to the development of these ideas and a basic framework could thus be enunciated in terms of the following:

1. The acceptance of the need to include in the exercise each and every state of the Persian Gulf littoral.
2. The establishment of a forum, official or non-official, for the conduct of a continuous and wide-ranging dialogue on the threat perception of each of the littoral states, and for exploring common means by which these security concerns could be addressed.
3. Implementation, simultaneously, of a set of commonly

---

[148]Martin, Lenore G. (ed.), *New Frontiers in Middle Security*, London, 1998, p. 7.
[149]*Common Security*, The Report of the Independent Commission on Disarmament and Security Issues under the Chairmanship of Olof Palme, (London 1982), pp. ix, 100.

accepted CBMs on the basis of a phased programme, taking care to ensure that the exercise does not begin by focusing on the mechanics of individual CBMs but by an overall review of the need for CBMs aimed at common understanding.

4. The dialogue should have for its basis a commitment of non-interference in the internal affairs of each other, respect for territorial integrity, settlement of border disputes and territorial claims on an equitable basis irrespective of the past history of such disputes, and cooperation and coordination of policies relating to hydrocarbon production and export as well as the initiation of steps for wider bilateral and regional economic cooperation, notwithstanding the complementary nature of the economies and the resultant limits to such cooperation. At some stage in the exercise, a regional or international convention on the freedom of navigation in the Straits of Hormuz could be put in place to guarantee the interests of oil producers and consumers.

The agenda, admittedly, was ambitious, given the tri-polar nature of the polarity in the Gulf. The most contentious problem would relate to the inclusion of Iraq; the alternative, of awaiting a change of regime, would defeat the very purpose of initiating a dialogue unrelated to value judgements concerning individual regimes. The question of CBMs too would raise problems of monitoring in relation to information imbalance, information sharing, and the role of third parties. Some of these could be addressed through new techniques of open-source intelligence (OSTINT) and knowledge management.[150] After the initial psychological barrier has been pierced, talks on arms control and regional security

---

[150]Rathmell, Andrew, 'Building Confidence in The Middle East', *Journal of Palestine Studies*, Vol. 29, No. 2, 2000, pp. 5–19.

could be initiated. In any such effort, the question of Iranian policies and intentions would loom large given the fears, doubts and suspicions prevalent in public and governmental circles in the GCC states. Any realistic assessment of the situation has to take note of these; for the same reason, however, it would be a folly to consider these perceptions as frozen in time and incapable of evolving. Detailed analysis, in fact, demonstrates the presence of a range of views relating to Iran in individual GCC capitals.[151]

The Saudi-Iranian détente, since 1997, is evidence enough of new thinking. Similar signals had emanated earlier from Oman, Qatar and Kuwait. On the Iranian side, Velayati's advocacy in 1994 of the concept of defensive security, and his suggestion for the establishment of a forum to discuss threat perceptions and security concerns[152] were followed by an offer in December 1995 to sign a non-aggression treaty with all the Persian Gulf states.[153] None of these has elicited a response. Some of these ideas could be pursued in the improved atmospherics in the region. The attitude of the UAE on the question of the islands, however, remains a major stumbling block and would require an innovative approach.

Yet another obstacle of substantial dimensions concerns the presence of foreign powers. They believed in Tehran, as it was at the time of the Shah, that 'the presence of foreign forces will not help to strengthen regional security but will, in itself, serve as an element of tension.' The GCC view, on the other

[151]Green, Jerrold D., 'Iran and Gulf Security', *Gulf Security in the Twenty-First Century*, David E. Long and Christian Koch (eds.), Abu Dhabi, 1997, p. 286 (n 4)—'Even in the Gulf, attitudes towards Iran are far more diverse than many realize, with different states having diverse views on and relations with Iran depending upon their individual circumstances.'

[152]1 September 1994 speech in the Conference on Disarmament. (CD/PV 690 pp. 8–14).

[153]Potter, Lawrence G., 'Confidence-Building Measures in The Persian Gulf', *The Persian Gulf at the Millennium*, Gary Sick and Lawrence G. Potter (eds.), New York, 1997.

hand, is that their security and that of the region is intimately connected to Western power-projection capability. These evidently contradictory postures can be reconciled only in the context of a changed political relationship between Iran and the United States, provided some progress is made in ending the ostracism of Iraq. If this were to come about or at least initiated, the US may see the need for a receding presence in the Gulf without detracting from the stability of the region and without jeopardizing its strategic interests.

In December 2004, in a conference co-sponsored in Bahrain by the IISS, London, the King of Bahrain called for a new security structure in the Gulf that would involve all its countries. In the same conference, the Saudi foreign minister drew attention to 'an urgent need for a collective effort aimed at developing a new and more solid framework for Gulf security'[154] having a national, a regional and an international component. The national component, he said, involved 'the urgent need for comprehensive reforms in our countries with some variation in the speed of implementation depending on the individual social conditions.' The regional framework 'should be based on four pillars: the GCC, Yemen, Iran and Iraq' and the international aspect of it should involve international guarantees, underwritten by the Security Council, for the sovereignty, independence and territorial integrity of all the littoral states. It also added that 'the international component of the suggested Gulf security framework should engage positively the emerging Asian powers as well, especially China and India.' This idea was not pursued.

[154]'India has a vital stake in peace and stability in this sub-region and in the security of the sea lanes connecting it to the outside world: Shri M. Hamid Ansari', Press Information Bureau, 10 October 2015, https://tinyurl.com/3tpp76vb. Accessed on 24 November 2025.

II

In geographical and strategic terms, the Persian Gulf is India's extended neighbourhood. Its value as a trade route was known since the earliest times. It was also the invasion route for early Arab expeditions to the western shores of the subcontinent. Its real political significance registered with the advent of the Portuguese in the first decade of the sixteenth century and was reinforced manyfold during the period of British dominance. The latter considered safeguarding of their political interests in the Persian Gulf absolutely essential for India's protection and, driven by the fear of Russian expansion, preferred a Persia divided into spheres of influence to a strong central government in Tehran.[155] In 1928, the Committee on Imperial Defence concluded that 'no foreign power must be allowed to establish a naval base or fortified post in the Gulf or air undertakings within striking distance of it.'[156]

In the initial period, independent India paid little attention to the Gulf region where British dominance continued till 1970. Nehru suspected an American hand in the ouster of Mossadeq in Iran in 1952. Apart from it, policy towards the Gulf 'tried to combine principles with practical considerations'; the latter included the need to counter Pakistan's effort to seek support on the J&K question. Relations with countries of the Persian Gulf littoral that joined Cold War military alliances were kept at a cool but correct level. Relations with Iraq improved considerably after the Revolution of 1958. Iranian perceptions relating to India changed only after the Bangladesh War.

There is no history of bilateral disputes between India and

---

[155]Tripathi, G.P., *Indo-Afghan Relations 1882-1907*, New Delhi, 1973, p. 113. Wilson, Arnold, *S.W. Persia: A Political Officer's Dairy 1907-1914*, London, 1941, p. 10.

[156]Morsy Abdullah, Mohammad. *The United Arab Emirates: A Modern History*, Croom Helm, London, 1978, p. 43.

the states of the Persian Gulf littoral. However, differences of perception in relation to India-Pakistan relations and concerning regional and global issues did arise from time to time and had an impact of varying degrees on political relationships. These related on the global plane to (a) India's policy of non-alignment, (b) India's objection to membership of military alliances, (c) India's friendship with the Soviet Union, and (d) some aspects of India's domestic economic policy. The Pakistan-specific issues were J&K, Indian Muslims, the East Pakistan situation resulting in the War of 1971, and questions relating to these that surfaced in the deliberations of the OIC since its inception in 1969. The approach of the individual states to these questions had an impact in some measure on the bilateral relations; in no case, however, was there any irreparable damage. The Indian response was to counter Pakistani moves, and to sustain a level of bilateral relations that would assist in the process. This also resulted in some duality of approach: 'Muslim countries, while temporizing on the Kashmir issue, and taking an impartial stand at the bilateral level with India, were collectively supportive of Pakistani position on Jammu and Kashmir. Such support found expression in OIC resolutions and in deliberations at the UN in New York and Geneva, and in the meetings of the Human Rights Commission' in the 1990s.[157]

A more proactive approach came with the first oil crisis of 1972–73 and the need to secure oil supplies as well as oil-related credits. The period 1973–78 witnessed a blossoming of political and economic relations with Iran. Relations were cultivated with Saudi Arabia, Kuwait, Qatar and the newly independent GCC states. The advent of an Indian workforce in the Gulf added a substantial economic dimension and their remittances became a welcome contribution to the foreign exchange-starved economy.

[157]Dixit, J.N., *Across Borders: Fifty Years of India's Foreign Policy*, Picus Books, New Delhi, 1998, pp. 248–249.

Changes in the global and regional situation at the end of the Cold War had a favourable impact on India's relations with the GCC states. The misunderstanding caused by the Indian position on Iraq in 1990–91, motivated principally by the desire to save and evacuate the Indian nationals in Kuwait, were quickly put aside; so was New Delhi's decision to establish diplomatic relations with Israel. The liberalization of the Indian economy and the new opportunities it offered were cautiously welcomed by the Gulf business communities.

Relations with Iran, after having touched a low point in 1989–90, were carefully nurtured and restored to normalcy. In this new approach, the focus of both governments was 'on complementarities of interests and concerns.'[158]

The imperatives of a relationship with the Gulf states today, and in the foreseeable future, can be identified with a fair degree of precision. The entire region is:

- Within the security parameter of India and the operating radius of the Indian Navy
- A principal source of imported hydrocarbon energy supplies
- A principal destination for manpower exports that provides employment to 3.5 million Indian nationals whose remittances exceed US$7 billion per annum
- A major trading partner with overall trade of over US$18 billion and growing
- An increasingly important destination for Indian projects and IT services

---

[158]Dixit, J.N., *My South Block Years: Memoirs of a Foreign Secretary*, UBS Publishers, New Delhi, 1996, p. 151. He makes the point (p. 153) that 'in overall terms Iran will always remain a cardinal factor affecting our Asian policies.' This became evident at the time of sending Indian assistance to the Northern Alliance in Afghanistan.

- India-friendly and Indian-friendly and desirous of enhancing its political, economic and technological interaction with India.

For each of these reasons, political stability and continued vibrancy in all parts of the Gulf are in India's interest. For the same reason, political and economic dislocation, induced by domestic or external factors, is not in the interest of India since such dislocations would have an adverse impact on the Indian economy and the well-being of a large number of Indian citizens.

At the turn of the century and despite the appearance of stability, any assessment of the Gulf situation seeks answers to a set of questions:

- How is the strategic stalemate in relation to Iraq to be addressed?
- How and on what terms would Iran's isolation from the West be ended?
- How to induce Gulf rulers, without destabilizing them, to renew their social contract with their citizens, initiate economic and political reforms, in order to address disenchantment and dissent among sections of their citizens?
- How to respond to the Islamization of perceptions in the Arab lands of the Gulf?
- In what manner would the Persian Gulf economies, being the principal suppliers of oil and gas, respond to the imperatives of globalization?

For India, countries in the Gulf are of prime economic, political and strategic importance and are the second largest trading partner after the US, with trade turnover of US$18,176 million annually. Two-thirds of India's oil imports are from this region, which not only has the advantage of geographical proximity, but also the quality of crude oil suits Indian refineries. Cooperation in the energy sector has been the hallmark of the ties with most of these countries and India is one of the biggest markets for energy products of these countries in the years to come.

The liberalization of Indian economy has yielded substantial benefits to the Gulf countries. According to the Ministry of Commerce, Government of India, GCC exports to India increased from $3,252.05 million in fiscal year 2003–04 to an estimated $6,900.80 million in 2004–05. Indian exports to GCC countries during the same period increased from $7,067.07 million to $9,536.69 million. UAE has the distinction of being the largest trading partner of India in the GCC followed by Saudi Arabia, Qatar, Kuwait, Bahrain and Oman. The GCC's biggest export to India is crude oil. The main product groups imported from India to GCC are agroproducts, textiles and garments, precious stones, building materials, plastic products, engineering goods, process plant and electrical equipment, manmade filaments/staple fibre, food products and miscellaneous goods.

A political dialogue was initiated when the foreign ministers of India and the GCC states met in New York on 26 September 2003. This was followed by the ministerial-level India-GCC Industrial Conference held in Mumbai on 17–18 February 2004. It endorsed the GCC-India Framework Agreement for Economic Cooperation and focused attention on four select priority areas in (a) trade, (b) investments, (c) industrial cooperation including small and medium enterprises/small-scale industries, and (d) transfer of technology including information technology. It welcomed the intention of the two sides to explore the possibility of an India-GCC Free Trade Area.

Some aspects of the policy approach were spelt out by Prime Minister Manmohan Singh in January 2005:

> Besides energy imports, there is also ample potential for

> India to evolve broader long-term economic relations with the region. This could include expanding our contacts with the Gulf Cooperation Council and other regional bodies into an enduring institutional relationship. We could also examine a more proactive strategy of seeking investments from West Asia, given India's emergence as an exciting and safe destination for foreign direct investment.[159]

The Indian economy's quest for 'massive doses of investment in every conceivable area' was underlined by the Prime Minister on the occasion of the Saudi King's visit to New Delhi in January 2006:

> Our requirement of foreign investment are particularly large in the field of power, telecommunications, roads, ports and housing sectors. Investment needs for the power and telecom sectors alone are estimated at over $100 billion over the next five years! Transport infrastructure, including airports and railways, will require another $55 billion over the next ten years. I therefore invite the business community of the Kingdom of Saudi Arabia to take advantage of these opportunities to further establish mutually beneficial joint venture projects.[160]

The message and the new areas of cooperation and investment identified in the Indo-Saudi Joint Declaration of 27 January 2006 are valid in equal measure for investors in other GCC counties.

The growing awareness of India in the GCC states is based on the realization that by 2010 India (a) will be the fourth largest economy in terms of PPP and the fourth largest consumer of energy in the world, (b) will be a major technology- and knowledge-based economy, and (c) with its renewed interest in

---

[159]Speech at Jamia Millia Islamia, inaugurating the Centre for West Asian Studies, 29 January 2005.

[160]Speech at the inauguration of the Saudi exhibition, 25 January 2006.

the Gulf, driven by necessity, ambition and opportunity, and by expanded security perspective, will be ready to contribute to the stability of the Gulf region by sharing its experience in maritime security and military training, and in combating terrorism.[161]

India's economic relationship with Iran is undergoing a change in view of the ever-changing international economic environment, which has an impact on both the countries, as it takes into account Iran's capabilities in the industrial sector. India's total trade for the year 2004–05 with Iran was of the value of $1,610.59 million (Indian exports $1,213.70 million, Indian imports $396.89 million).

In case of Iraq, and in the context of the disturbed conditions there, the value of total trade is limited to $129.59 million (Indian exports $128.49 million). Once normalcy returns to Iraq, the strength of the economic relationship between the two countries would be appropriately reflected.

III

Overall, a study of the Persian Gulf littoral will require a segment-wise analysis of the following:

1. **GCC Countries:** In the foreseeable future, these will constitute an area of stability for the following reasons: (a) there are modest pressures for calibrated political change and no impulse to upset the apple cart by seeking revolutionary or violent change; (b) there is enhanced economic prosperity, though unevenly distributed; and (c) member countries are on good terms with the United Sates and G-8, are getting integrated in the global economy, and are crucial for its prosperity. Internal stability in Saudi Arabia and the pace of reforms in Saudi society would continue to raise concerns,

[161]Sager, Abdulaziz, 'Strategic Roadmap for Robust Saudi-India Ties', 22 January 2006.

though not alarm. On the other hand, Iraq and Iran will constitute areas of actual or potential instability though not for the same set of reasons. With regard to both of these, much will depend on the US-Iranian relationship. It is difficult to make a prediction about it since domestic politics in both countries, as well as the shadow of US-Israeli relations, will continue to influence it disproportionately. Another indeterminate is Iraq, its cohesiveness, and the nature of its central government.

The nature of changes in these countries needs to be assessed in social, economic, political and strategic segments. Gradual and calibrated social change, driven by the youth-bulge in the population, would result in partial and uneven modernization. Wealth would continue to be generated but critical decisions about its most productive use would be contested in increasing measure. The impulse for good and participatory governance would register modest success but would not change the monarchical character of the GCC regimes or of the Islamic republic in Iran. The shape of American hegemony would be critically influenced by the course of events in Iraq and the manner of a US withdrawal. Security in the Gulf would become, in increasing measure, a matter of global concern. Asian countries like Japan, China and India would signal greater interest in arrangements for the security of the sea lanes but may eschew Western suggestions for participation in operations to secure the hinterland.

2. **Iraq:** In view of the prevailing anarchy there and the imponderables introduced by it, it is not possible to prognosticate in general terms. Different outcomes would need to be assessed: (a) Iraq with a meaningful central authority; (b) a united Iraq but with all effective power in the hands of three regional/ethnic units; (c) emergence of three international entities from the ruins of present-day Iraq.

In the first case, Iraq would be in a position to endorse and sanctify the 1975 border agreement with Iran and the 1993 Security Council-declared border with Kuwait. Eschewing the territorial and political ambitions of the Baath years, it may respond meaningfully to a cooperative security regime in the Gulf and also make itself a factor in the geopolitics of the region. It could use the oil resources of northern and southern parts of the country to make Iraq a major source of oil supplies to the world once again. These considerations would be operative, but with lesser intensity and success in the second case. The third possibility, on the other hand, would generate wholly new impulses that may satisfy Iran and Kuwait, alarm Saudi Arabia and Turkey, tempt Jordan or Syria and have an impact on Arab psyche that is difficult to assess. Its overall impact may be wide-ranging destabilization for many years.

3. **Iran:** What would be the direction of changes in Iran and its impact on countries of the region? The reformist period of post-Khomeini Iran came to an abrupt end in June 2005 when the neo-conservative Ahmadinejad defeated Rafsanjani by a convincing margin. The electorate, predominantly under 30, belied domestic and external prognosis that its choice would lie between the advocates of democracy and human rights and the advocates of reform. As a result, the principal organs of the state are now in the control of the conservatives; by the same token, reformist opposition of all shades is now essentially outside the system. Immediately after the installation of the new president, Iran was confronted by the impasse in nuclear negotiations in the IAEA. This, and Ahmadinejad's demagogy, have resulted in Iran's diplomatic isolation. The nuclear issue has aroused a nationalist fervour that seems to have subdued the public's demand for the fulfilment of electoral promises. Both sets of developments have created a precarious balance

that can be upset by a number of unanticipated happenings. There is, however, no threat to the political system or to domestic stability. Discontent is essentially economic; the high level of oil prices has helped mitigate it.

By virtue of its size, population and political orientation, Iran looms large over the Gulf horizon. The GCC states are apprehensive as well as careful in their attitude and dealings with Iran. Many of them (e.g. Dubai in UAE) have large Iranian communities and substantial commercial interests in the relationship. They do not want a nuclear Iran, nor do they relish a destabilized Iran since the consequences of change or attempted change there cannot be anticipated. The lessons of Iraq weigh heavily on their minds.

4. **Saudi stability and reforms and its impact on energy and employment:** Three developments in the past 12 months have had a favourable impact on Saudi Arabia: (a) restoration of close ties with the US, (b) King Abdullah's commitment to continue calibrated reforms, and (c) Saudi rejection of Takfiri trend in Islam and gains in combating local terrorism. The Kingdom would remain critical to the world's demand for crude oil, but with limited spare capacity. At the same time, the terrorist attempt to attack Abqaiq (as the earlier attempt on Ras Tanura) shows the vulnerability of the country to non-traditional threats. The question of youth unemployment is being addressed; a judgement on the extent of its success cannot yet be made. Relations with Iran continue to be nurtured carefully. The principal national security concern is now the cohesion of Iraq.
5. **Future security architecture of PG:** Imperatives of regime security would propel continuance of existing arrangements, while the demonstrated limits of the US hegemony will induce exploratory ventures in seeking options. The temptation of a cooperative security paradigm, as also of the involvement of

more external powers, would induce thinking on alternatives. A great deal would depend on the future of US-Iran relations; a measure of normalization would introduce a wholly new dynamics.

6. **Role of religion in society and politics:** The countries of the Gulf littoral are Muslim societies and subscribe to Muslim religious and social ethos. The GCC countries, given their tribal origins, have moved from traditional patriarchy to modern patriarchy (*neo-patriarchy*) and thus exhibit a schizophrenic personality. Islam remains a major source of legitimacy for the rulers and a uniting bond with their populace. In the period after 1990 and principally propelled by returnees from Afghanistan, Islamism, defined by Olivier Roy as 'a socio-cultural movement embodying the protest and frustration of a generation of youth that has not been integrated socially or politically,' made some headway. The traditional *ulema*, however, remained aligned to the ruling establishments. Post-9/11 developments have reduced the appetite for violence and induced many of these groups to work within their respective political systems but in an increasingly Islamized discourse. This trend is likely to continue.

   In Iraq, the most outwardly secular society in the Gulf before the invasion of 2003, religious *and* sectarian identity has now become integral at individual and group levels. Iran remains a rich and powerful source of innovative ideas on Islamic thinking of the Shia school about society and politics. The present political dispensation, however, is disinclined towards them.

7. **Role of major external powers and of NATO:** Given the totality of strategic and economic interests, the interests of external powers would remain undiminished. This is borne out by recent NATO pronouncements. Apart from the G-8 and other Western powers, India, China and South Korea, as

principal beneficiaries of Gulf energy resources and markets, would raise their political profile in the area and would be encouraged by many of the littoral states to do so.

8. **Implications of higher oil prices:** In a testimony before the US Foreign Relations Committee on 30 March 2006, the Executive Director of the Energy Modelling Forum of Stanford University stated that 'the odds of a foreign oil disruption happening over the next 10 years are slightly higher than 80 percent.'[162] The riskiest areas were identified as the Persian Gulf, Nigeria and Venezuela. Such a disruption 'would remove at least two million barrels per day—an amount representing at least 2.1 percent of expected global oil production,' and have serious consequences for the US economy since a doubling of oil prices could result in a decline of real GNP by anything between 2 and 5 per cent. (The model developed for this study excluded any release of oil from the US strategic petroleum reserve.)

   The Persian Gulf and Nigeria account for 70 and 15 per cent, respectively, of total Indian oil imports. A doubling or near-doubling of oil prices resulting from a global shortage would, therefore, impact India adversely since calculations suggest that a US$10 increase in oil price could reduce GDP by one per cent. This burden would be unavoidable in the short run; over a longer period, however, energy conservation and rationalization of energy use, suggested in the Parikh Report of the Planning Commission, may offer correctives.

9. **Pakistan's role:** This could be visualized in (a) strategic and (b) economic terms in relation to India. There is little or no prospect of the re-emergence of the Pak-Saudi or Pak-UAE military relationship of an earlier period since perceptions

[162]'The Hidden Cost of Oil', *GovInfo*, 30 March 2006, https://tinyurl.com/56ybzdfz. Accessed on 24 November 2025.

and requirements have changed. In the foreseeable future, Pakistan's strategic role could only be supportive of the wider US role and that too would be constrained both by Pakistan's domestic considerations and by the India factor in the local and global calculus. GCC countries would continue to channel funds for 'charity' in the direction of official and non-official recipients in Pakistan but these would be within the post-9/11 security framework. GCC states would remain wary of Islamist forces emerging from Pakistan. On the economic front, Pakistan would play a low-profile role—as supplier of skilled workforce and in some export sectors—in these burgeoning economies. Its efforts to influence local thinking in relation to India are unlikely to make headway in view of the conscious decision taken by all the GCC states, and particularly by Saudi Arabia, to delink their relations with the two South Asian neighbours. A different scenario, however, may emerge in the event of an Indo-Pak conflict when public opinion and emotive factors may propel a change of direction, however transitory.

10. **India's core interests and ways to further them:** India's core interests in the Gulf would remain riveted on (a) supplies of crude oil and gas in increasing measure, (b) expanding the market for exports of goods, services and technology, and remaining open to a changing mix in the export basket, (c) remaining a principal source of semi-skilled, skilled and professional workforce and an important recipient of foreign exchange remittances, (d) remaining sensitive to the changing skills-requirement of the market and preparing public opinion for these changes, (e) sustaining and developing good and cooperative relations with each of the littoral states as well as with the GCC as a trading entity, (f) sensitizing the Gulf states on a continuous basis to India's potential as a major market to their primary exports as also to their investments,

(g) projecting in an unobtrusive manner India's strategic interests and capabilities, including the capacity to protect sea lanes, (h) preventing the emergence of hostile powers or combinations in the Gulf region, and (i) avoiding involvement in regional or extra-regional military ventures directed against a littoral state of the Persian Gulf.

11. **External factors.** This period has coincided with an enormous enhancement in the economic and strategic relevance of the Gulf. In the foreseeable future, its oil and gas resources will be critical to meeting the world's growing appetite for energy. According to the International Energy Agency, 'its share of world oil production would jump from 35% in 2004 to 44% in 2030.'

    The Persian Gulf is an area of opportunity for an India that is beginning to register its presence in economic and strategic terms. It could also be a source of dislocations, even problems. A closer monitoring of the developments in the region, and of the interplay of global forces at work there, is thus of relevance to India's strategic planning.

Parts of this were originally written in 2000 in the Occasional Paper Series of the Centre of West Asian Studies, JNU, and as Chapter 13 of India's Foreign Policy: Challenges and Opportunities (Foreign Service Institute, New Delhi, 2007), and supplemented by notes from discussions.

Chapter 27

India at 2047

Allow me to recall what Jawaharlal Nehru said in the Constituent Assembly on 4 December 1947: 'Whatever policy we may lay down, the art of conducting the foreign affairs of a country lies in finding out what is most advantageous to the country.' This, in the terminology of our times, came to be defined as national interest, which translates itself into a hierarchy of interests, to be secured by a policy that is the sum total of the principles, interests and objectives formulated by a state in conducting its relations with other states in the global community. Its contents were thus both general and specific.

This grand strategy therefore has to be a judicious mix of principles, interests and objectives. While the challenges are evident, ideas in embryonic shape exist and need to be developed. They must at all times be sufficiently flexible to accommodate changing external and domestic requirements and capabilities, yet principled enough to look tenable to the audience, be it domestic opinion or affected targets. It must above all be credible in terms of intentions and capabilities. Strategic atrophy has to be avoided. The acme of skill, says the ancient formula, is 'to subdue the enemy without fighting.'

The international environment of the post-World War II period was characterized by the Cold War and power blocs. This was not perceived to be in our interest. India, instead, articulated a temper of peace and friendship with all countries. Non-alignment was the logical outcome and, having fought against colonial domination, we empathized with others seeking the same outcome. Decolonization was thus accorded high priority in our global agenda and we went on to play a major role in the process that followed.

To begin with, what are the principal interests of any state to be promoted and protected? They, of necessity, begin with independence and territorial integrity. The first requires sovereignty that, in theory at least, implies giving orders to all and receiving orders from none. Its claimant must feel secure, defined by Walter Lippman in terms that bear repetition: 'A nation is secure to the extent to which it is not in danger of having to sacrifice core values, if it wishes to avoid war, and is able, if challenged, to maintain them by such victory in such a war.' This security has military and non-military dimensions.

India is a democratic republic with pluralism and secularism being its essential concomitants. The first three essential interests on which challenges have to be met and countered are thus Independence, Territorial Integrity and Core Values, and while there cannot be a dispute on the first two, contemporary debate in our country on the third tends to question, even dilute, what is supposedly settled. It is enshrined in the principles enunciated in the Preamble of the Constitution of India and specifically on *equality, justice* and *fraternity*. A mere formal acceptance of these, however, is insufficient and must be accompanied by a *commitment* to them in actual practice. This has to be to the exclusion of other principles sought to be included on grounds of faith or culture.

Alongside are the targets to achieve in political, economic, developmental, technological and cultural spheres. These too have national and global dimensions. They are essentially state-centric exercises and are spelt out in President of India's address to Parliament, in Niti Ayog and other development plans, and premised to some extent on the UN Sustainable

Development Agenda 2030. A sociological perspective would however necessitate more comprehensive, category-specific social-inclusion development targets. They necessitate Rule of Law and functioning instrumentalities of governance.

DEFINING OUR CHALLENGES

To me therefore, the first big challenge has to be political cohesion and social harmony since without them life of citizens would be nasty, brutish and short, and devoid of peace and development. The first necessitates the sustenance of what Article I of the Constitution describes as the Union of States. Given the historical context, the focus of the framers was on national unity and integrity resulting in a highly centralized federation.

The functioning of the polity over seven decades has however resulted in 'a counter-productive over-centralization' and given rise to the view that there is need for restructuring to make it more viable and resilient to promote effective centre-state relations and federal practices across the country whose democratic decision-making will bring forth different political combinations in federal units.

The expression 'cooperative federalism' has found its way in the vocabulary of political leaders but without overcoming the imperatives of majoritarian politics that pulls it in an opposite direction. Another implication of this, in external relations, has been pointed out in an op-ed a few days back.

Alongside, there is visible erosion in the functioning of institutions and the enforcement of Rule of Law. Both sets of correctives are imperative.

No less relevant to the proper functioning of the democratic system is social harmony which is often under stress and whose principal victims are the minority and underprivileged segments of the public. This may, and does, serve a party-political purpose but is invariably detrimental to social cohesion. The antithesis of social cohesion is *anarchy* whose twin consequences were foreseen as early as the Mahabharata, where it is said that 'a kingdom in which anarchy prevails becomes weak and is soon afflicted by robbers' and cannot have righteousness.

Recent years have witnessed periodic unrest in segments of our public emanating from socioeconomic distress. The ongoing farmers' agitation is a hard example. The Shaheen Bagh protest last year was another. There is evidence of similar expressions of distress arising from grievances in tribal communities within the country and on borders.

Once political cohesion and social harmony are secured, the state apparatus has to focus on development for public good. Social inclusion, public health, and environment are the obvious priorities. Recent experience highlights the deficiencies on each of these counts. The size of our polity and its cultural heterogeneity make a compelling case for federalization in practice.

Thus political cohesion, social inclusion, harmony, public health and environment would together result in a healthier Republic of India on the eve of its centenary in 2047. India's destiny is in its own hands and through a sustained 9–10 per cent annual growth, it can make the transition from poverty to affluence in one generation.

It would also have hopefully attained the 'norms of righteousness' set out in its foundational document and delivered to its people a fair degree of material prosperity through it.

These then are the 'domestic roots' for our foreign policy whose primary objective is to secure them in the best manner possible. In terms of formal jurisdiction and practice, this and related subjects (items 10–20 in the Union List) are covered in the Seventh Schedule of Article 246 of the Constitution.

FORGING BEYOND BORDERS

A word about the craft of conducting foreign relations is relevant. Masters ancient and modern have spoken about the need to seek credible mechanisms for dialogue and to seek in them minimum areas of agreement resulting in what has been called 'patient accumulation of partial successes.' Our own experience of over seven decades would sustain this. It becomes more relevant in our times and in the context of a developing view that the 21st century will mature in a world mired in perpetual chaos, into durable disorder which will contain rather than solve problems.

A practical and philosophical question about national security needs to be answered. What is or should be its purpose—to secure India and develop India as it exists towards its ideals, or to divert its energies to dominate its neighbours? The first requires cooperation and the second domination. The approach for both would not be identical. An option for cooperation would nevertheless necessitate an adequate capacity to address transgressions.

India has a population of 1.3 billion. Its demographic mix itself is daunting: over 4,635 communities, 78 per cent of which are not only linguistic and cultural but social categories. Its religious minorities constitute 19.4 per cent of the population, of whom Muslims account for 14.2 per cent. The human diversities are both hierarchical and special. The de jure 'we' is, in reality, fragmented and divided by yawning gaps that remain to be bridged; hence the need for social cohesion and inclusion.

There is talk at times of Greater India and of the glory of a distant, imagined past. Will this, in terms of territory or population or both, assist or hamper this process?

According to the Annual Report of the Ministry of Home Affairs, India has 15,106.7 km of land border and 7,500 km of sea border. A feature of our land borders is that major or minor points of contention have persisted with regard to borders with Bangladesh, China and Pakistan, and attempts to resolve them continue with many limitations and varying degrees of success. This, consequently, has remained a significant challenge in the conduct of foreign relations with neighbours and has at times resulted in armed conflicts with varying results. The alternative, of a meaningful framework for effective cooperation on the basis of equality and mutual benefit, is yet to crystallize.

Either way, national security within existing borders becomes the first objective of foreign policy. The wherewithal for it is the national security apparatus to counter formal and non-conventional threats. This cannot be so in isolation since India is part of the global community and contributes to its ideals and objectives. Hence, importance is attached, since its inception, to diplomacy and the structure and activities of the United Nations and other multilateral agencies.

Any set of policies have two ingredients: principles and practices. The principles of Indian foreign policy were spelt out in early years and were focused on non-alignment with power blocs and autonomy in decision-making. Problems with neighbours of necessity assumed primacy but not at the expense of wider issues of global concern—war and peace, regional conflicts, decolonization in Africa—and in each of these India played a role of significance. The Korean War and the role played by Nehru to end the war is an early example. President Truman's comment on it is noteworthy: 'Nehru has sold us down the Hudson. His attitude has been responsible for us losing the war in Korea.' In a sense, India defined itself in opposition to the Cold War and focused its international energies on the Non-Alignment Movement.

Today the global scene stands transformed. Two decades of the 21st century have witnessed changes in power structures. As with earlier bipolarity, unipolarity too has collapsed. The United States, despite the size of its economy and technological superiority, is a retreating power. Europe has discovered its strength in a non-homogenous European Union. The Soviet Union has been replaced by Russia and a number of its erstwhile units are seeking their own place in the sun, unsure of their affinity to the former arrangement. The Arab world, linguistic affinity apart, hardly agrees on any core unifying agenda. Israel has succeeded in securing its place in the sub-region.

For us, the priority has to be immediate proximity. China is a neighbour with whom we have a long border with disputed segments as well as environmental issues of a complex nature. It is militarily and economically stronger. There have been periods of military confrontation followed by commitments to maintain the status quo. There exists a vibrant trading relationship, adverse yet beneficial to segments of our economy.

China's economic progress is dazzling; its political structure and social cohesion are impressive. Its plans to expand influence on land and sea are at times unnerving. Yet, the outside world is barely aware of its diversities and its domestic tensions.

It is nowadays felt that in view of new challenges, particularly in maritime security, India's active participation in Quad would accrue strategic benefits. Here, two questions arise. What is the nature of threats faced by us and to what extent will it be addressed by Quad? Secondly, would it enhance or lessen our freedom for strategic options?

Another obvious example is Pakistan. Here the subjective is as relevant as the objective. The legacy of 1947 and perceptions emanating from it remain relevant in varying degrees with actors and spectators, and has caused occasional glee and more frequent sorrow. Despite political and economic disparities, it is a nuclear power and uses this status to its benefit.

Other areas of tensions relate to water and boundary disputes with Bangladesh and the complex question of Tamil citizens of Sri Lanka. None of these have been resolved and all remain subject of patient negotiations within frameworks of commitment to cooperation for mutual benefit. A complex set of considerations influence relations with Nepal.

In a wider sense, the global order has changed and thrown up new challenges. The expectation that the UN system will become more democratic and egalitarian has not materialized but new platforms for focused cooperation on a range of matters relating to human survival have come forth and nations are being compelled to participate in them seriously.

While priorities in foreign policy of any country cannot be done sequentially, precedence or ordering is unavoidable, more so because problem areas are seldom single-issue ones. The same holds for problems that transcend national borders and are regional in nature. Thus, with neighbours, matters of war and peace and human survival cannot be deferred or put on the backburner. In each of these and in actual practice, a nation's own ideals on bilateral or global problems inevitably play a role.

Policymaking begins with specific, immediate and medium-term objectives. A developing country like India seeks external assistance, technology and technology transfer, and expertise in different ways and at different times. These have to be identified along with resources. Thereafter, they get moulded in a policy framework and pursued through professional and political initiatives. Room is made for setbacks and the challenge at all times is to accommodate setbacks in a wider framework of continuing cooperation.

India is a status quo power and does not seek territories of others. It is also committed to working for a peaceful world and a peaceful South Asia. Doubts about these commitments are sought to be raised by some, relating to the happenings of 1947, to our being the successor state to the British Indian Empire, to our 'map or no map' statement, and to the stages through which a boundary problem became a boundary dispute with unfortunate consequences.

Recent happenings worldwide have shown that problems beyond human and governmental control have arisen on account of pandemics, water resources and environmental degradation and climate change. None of these can be addressed nationally; each requires united global responses, each needs to transcend traditional patterns of voluntary commitments, and instead be based on maximum capacity commitment. New technologies must not be monopolized.

The five big ideas for foreign policy should therefore be related to the following: (i) national security with regional boundary and water disputes, (ii) regional cooperation, (iii) pandemics, (iv) environmental degradation, and (v) climate change.

The foregoing should not be seen as the rant of a pessimist but a realistic reading of the present and the foreseeable future.

This was an address delivered by the former Vice President of India on 30 May 2021, organized virtually by the Council for Strategic and Defense Research in New Delhi.

Acknowledgements

Modern publishers have multiple responsibilities. These also shed light on the intricate relationship between the author and the publisher. There are also rare instances, like that of the American author George Ade, when these deteriorate and propel the author to become their own publisher.

I have to place on record my thanks to Shri Kapish Mehra of Rupa Publications for the arrangement of the publication of this book, and also to Ms Yamini Chowdhury, Ms Richa Tewari and Ms Padma Pegu for their strenuous efforts in editing the text at various times. The assistance of my colleague Shri Anil Kaushik was invaluable.

Index